THE DEATH OF
KING
ARTHUR

THE DEATH OF
KING
ARTHUR

A NEW VERSE TRANSLATION

Simon Armitage

W. W. NORTON & COMPANY

NEW YORK   LONDON

Copyright © 2012 by Simon Armitage

The text of the *Alliterative Morte Arthure* printed alongside Simon Armitage's translation is taken from the book *King Arthur's Death* edited by Larry D. Benson, published by the University of Exeter Press (new edition 1986, 9780859892674).

For information about permission to reproduce selections from this book, write to Permissions, W. W. Norton & Company, Inc., 500 Fifth Avenue, New York, NY 10110

For information about special discounts for bulk purchases, please contact W. W. Norton Special Sales at specialsales@wwnorton.com or 800-233-4830

Manufacturing by RR Donnelley, Harrisonburg, VA
Book design by JAM Design
Production manager: Anna Oler

Library of Congress Cataloging-in-Publication Data

Morte Arthure. English & English (Middle English)
The death of King Arthur : a new verse translation / Simon Armitage. — 1st ed.
    p. cm.
"The text of the *Alliterative Morte Arthure* printed alongside Simon Armitage's translation is taken from the book *King Arthur's Death* edited by Larry D. Benson, published by the University of Exeter Press (new edition 1986 . . .") — T. p. verso.
ISBN 978-0-393-07397-3 (hardcover)
1. Kings and rulers—Poetry. 2. Arthurian romances.
I. Armitage, Simon, 1963– II. Title.
PR2065.M3A325 2012
821'.1—dc22

                    2011038278

W. W. Norton & Company, Inc.
500 Fifth Avenue, New York, N.Y. 10110
www.wwnorton.com

W. W. Norton & Company Ltd.
Castle House, 75/76 Wells Street, London W1T 3QT

1 2 3 4 5 6 7 8 9 0

CONTENTS

INTRODUCTION

I N A D 410 the Romans withdrew from Britain, leaving the country open to attack from Germanic tribes all along Europe's northwestern fringes. The pullout was a gradual process rather than a moonlight flit, but for history to make sense it requires eras and periods separated by memorable dates and clear dividing lines rather than vague segues or blurred transitions. Viewed in those terms, it was as if the Romans had left overnight. A period of huge social turmoil was to follow, but with very little in the way of evidence or record, and it is in the shadowy, silent days of the next hundred or so years that the first glimmers and rumors of a character called Arthur are to be found.

Through the deep roots of Welsh folklore Arthur initially makes his name as a Celtic hero, defending the embattled people of the west of Britain against a variety of enemies, including the English. One of the earliest mentions of him comes in the poem *Y Gododdin,* possibly predating the ninth century, in which another warlord is singled out for praise, despite being "no Arthur," suggesting that Arthur's fame and qualities were already widely known and needed little in the way of explanation. Arthur appears in other Welsh stories, some not written down till the turn of the first millennium but with their origins dating back to a much earlier age. In the ninth-century *Historia Brittonum,* sometimes attributed to a Welsh monk, Nennius, we get the earliest "historical" account of Arthur in action. The text describes a series of twelve battles, culminating in the Battle of Badon Hill, in which Arthur is said to have killed 960 men in one day by his own hand. Similarly, in the *Annales Cambriae,* composed not later than the tenth century, the author presents as a true historical occurrence the Battle of Camlann, during which the fatal fight between Arthur and Mordred takes place.

In 1136, Geoffrey of Monmouth created the first "biography" of King Arthur in a section of his *History of the Kings of Britain,* written in Latin. At a time when literature and history were not necessarily approached as independent disciplines, Geoffrey positions Arthur in a succession of British monarchs dating right back to Brutus. It was a popular and cleverly conceived text, pleasing to the ruling Norman elite, and one that offered a unifying and rousing version of Arthur that appealed both to Norman aspirations and to the Welsh tradition.

A poet from Jersey, Wace, introduced the concept of the Round Table in his *Roman de Brut* (1155), and not long afterward Arthur was to receive something of a total makeover at the hands of Chrétien de Troyes, the brilliant French author of several Arthurian Romances. In keeping with the literary fashions and social tastes of the day, ideals of courtly love and chivalric code became the all important themes, with Arthur sidelined, emasculated even, by the deeds of the amorous Lancelot in pursuit of Guinevere and the adventurous Perceval in pursuit of the Holy Grail. In these stories, honor, faith, and virtue became both motive and subject, and it is interesting to consider the extent to which the popular image of King Arthur, one of Britain's greatest national heroes, is in a good part the creation of French-speaking poets.

Sometime around the end of the twelfth century, a Worcestershire parish priest by the name of Layamon wrote the long, sprawling poem *Brut,* an important moment not only in the transmission of Arthurian narrative but for English literature in general, since it was the first time that the story of Arthur had been written in the English language. Layamon drew heavily on Wace, just as Wace had drawn on Geoffrey of Monmouth, just as Geoffrey had drawn on the Welsh myths, but plagiarism, or "intertextuality" as we might allow these days, was not only considered necessary and acceptable but often looked on as a badge of learning. Nowhere is this form of compositing more evident or successful than in the work of Sir Thomas Malory, the author of the prose work *Le Morte Darthur,* as published by Caxton in 1485. Possibly written during Malory's incarceration, the book is a classic of world literature and the text by which most people have come to know the stories of King Arthur and the Knights of the Round Table. Malory's achievement was to pull together many disparate and sometimes confusing strands of Arthurian legend and present them as one definitive and continuous storyline, and to do so in a style that had all the excitement of fiction but also the gravitas of fact. The sword in the stone, the lady of the lake, Guinevere's adultery with Lancelot: all these scenes and plots have their origins elsewhere, but it is through Malory's retelling that they have become so ingrained in our consciousness and have remained so popular.

Malory had certainly read the *Alliterative Morte Arthure* (*AMA*), the academic and unglamorous title given to the nearly four and a half thousand line poem written sometime around 1400, of which this book is a translation. Its title distinguishes it from another poem of the same era written in lyrical eight-line verses, known as the *Stanzaic Le Morte Arthur,* and both poems could be considered part of a renewed flourishing in Arthurian literature, which included *Sir Gawain and the Green Knight.* Like *Gawain,* the *AMA* was written by an anonymous author and only one copy remains in existence, kept in the gatehouse library of Lincoln Cathedral. Because of dialect words and certain turns of phrase the author is thought to have come from the northeast midlands or possibly the north of England, though the manuscript is actually a copy, in the hand of the Yorkshireman, Robert Thornton, who may well have contributed some of his own literary and linguistic mannerisms to the poem's style and tenor. Both *Gawain* and the *AMA* are written in alliterating lines that harped back to the Anglo-Saxon style of poetic composition, but unlike *Gawain,* whose plotline hinges around one moment of jaw-dropping magic, the *AMA* concerns itself with the far more down-to-earth world of warfare and politics, specifically the ever-topical matter of Britain's relationship with continental Europe, and the no less relevant subject of its military interests overseas. During the Christmas celebrations at Carlisle, the festivities of the Round Table are rudely interrupted by a messenger from the Roman Emperor, Lucius Iberius, demanding taxes and homage from Arthur in respect of disputed territories in France and elsewhere. Rising to the challenge,

Arthur and his army embark on an armed campaign that takes them almost to the gates of Rome, before Arthur is forced to turn back to deal with matters closer to home.

The *Alliterative Morte Arthure* is hardly a story of suspense, since its outcome is announced in its very title, but the manner of the King's death and the way in which every incident right from the opening passages are bound up in its conclusion are examples of sophisticated literary structure and storytelling at its very best. The tale also incorporates several subplots describing the fates of dozens of fighters on both sides of the battle lines, including Gawain himself, no longer the callow, naive wanderer outwitted by a green wizard and a wrinkled witch, but a fearsome warrior and Arthur's most trusted knight. Nevertheless, three episodes are remarkable for their vivid flights of fancy. The first describes in the most graphic detail a battle to the death between King Arthur and a hideous, cannibalistic giant occupying Mont Saint-Michel on the French coast, who counts the beards of famous kings among his grisly trophies. The other two are prophetic nightmares at the beginning then at the end of Arthur's European campaign. In the first, a monstrous bear from the east does battle with a massive dragon from the west, and in the second, the King is wooed then turned upon by an all powerful lady as she spins Fortune's Wheel. These dream sequences are internalized, private glimpses into the conflicted mind of Arthur, in stark contrast with the rhetorical world of court and the cut and thrust of war. Through them, we begin to see Arthur as a human being rather than just a figurehead, and consequently his fate becomes a matter of huge drama and poignancy.

In and among, fight follows fight, charge follows charge, and the poem itself is a battlefield littered with horribly disfigured corpses and no end of internal organs. Once the bowing and the trading of witty insults had been dispensed with, medieval warfare was a gruesome business, and the author of the *AMA* doesn't seek to spare us from the details. In the heat of these battles, and at the heart of the story, stands Arthur, King of Britain and indisputably the central character of this very English poem. By contrast, Lancelot has only a walk-on part, and Arthur is restored from his peripheral role in the

French Romances to take center stage. It is Arthur's fate that hangs in the balance, and if Arthur should fall then the Round Table and the country will fall with him; nothing less than the future of Britain is at stake. With Arthur's demise, the author seems to be telling us what we already know, that all things must come to pass, and on that level the poem is a solid reinforcement of the inevitability of change. But there is also a moral dimension to Arthur's fate, in which actions have their eventual consequences. When Arthur embarks on his military undertaking there is a sense of a wrong being righted, the prosecution of a war in the name of justice and honor. But when he struts about, godlike, on the walls of Metz without armor or shield we catch a glimpse of a man who has started to believe in his infallibility and immortality. As his forces push violently and without mercy into Tuscany and begin eying the bigger prize of Rome itself, personal glory appears to be the motive, coupled with boastfulness and pride, and it is at this moment that Fortune's Wheel must turn.

There are many challenges facing the translator of this poem. For all the candle-lit hours that the original scribe worked on what must have been a labor of love, certain words or even lines are, or have become, indecipherable, and a relative lack of punctuation leads to ambiguity and in some cases contradiction when trying to follow the progression of thought or the structure of an argument. Stock phrases and alliterative formulations are repeated again and again; to the medieval mind they might have provided a kind of reassuring continuity or even the glue by which the story hung together, but to the contemporary reader they often seem slack or unnecessary. For example, I can only assume that the soldiers of Genoa are "giants" not because of some geo-specific DNA coding that enhanced their physical stature but because Genoa and giant happen to share the same consonant. The sheer number of characters is also a complication, some of whom appear to have been created only for alliterative convenience, and some of whom have very similar names despite fighting for different armies. The author of the manuscript obviously found the cast list somewhat confusing as well. At line 1433 Sir Berill appears to have died (at the very least he is "borne down") in a Roman counterattack, only to be found escorting the prisoner convoy at line 1605 and to be killed once more by the King of Libya in the Cutting of Clime, wherever that might be. Likewise, in the original, Sir Bedivere seems to have been buried first in Bayonne and then just a few lines later in Burgundy, just prior to Sir Cador being buried in Caen, only to be found standing at Arthur's side nearly two thousand lines later ready to ride into battle with Mordred. Even the Emperor Lucius isn't immune from this kind of apparent inconsistency. At lines 2076–2079 he is speared by Lancelot, the lance entering his hip, passing through his stomach to protrude from his back by several inches, but by line 2220 he is fighting fit once again. I hesitate to say that these moments reflect lapses of concentration on behalf of the scribe since it is possible they have some deeper textual relevance, but rightly or wrongly I have tried to devise unobtrusive strategies to make sense of the most glaringly contradictory material, and I hope readers will forgive me my own errors of judgment where they have inevitably occurred. For reference, I have included a list of characters, and might well have attached an atlas of medieval Europe as well, though it has to be remembered that the *AMA* contains as many speculations about the "real world" as it does about the world of fantasy, and that the original author's "map" should not necessarily be used for navigational purposes.

Typically, each line of the original has four stresses, two falling either side of a caesura, and contains three alliterating syllables, usually two on the left side of the divide then one on the right, followed by an unalliterating stressed syllable, a pattern that might be represented by the equation *xx/xy*. So for example:

"I am comen frọ the conquerour,   courtais and gentle,"   987

But other patterns exist within the poem, and some lines show no demonstrable alliteration at all, offering the contemporary translator a level of flexibility or leeway when it comes to reengineering the poem's acoustics. It should also be noted that all vowels and the letter aitch share the same alliterative value in poems such as this, and I have happily followed suit. I have also attempted, where meaning and diction would allow, to imitate the original poet's habit of continuing the same alliteration over several lines, like a kind of knowingly extravagant riff. The practice is unusual and something of a trademark quality of the *AMA*; it gives us a sense of a poet reveling in the playfulness of language and not embarrassed by the range of his vocabulary.

The original is inconsistent in its use of section breaks or what we might loosely describe as verses, so to open the poem up and make it easier on the eye I have added my own breaks and indents where it seemed appropriate. And one further imposition: after much deliberation, I took the decision to present this translation entirely in the past tense, when the original fluctuates between past and historical present. The present tense clearly helps to activate and animate certain scenes, and I had assumed at one stage that its usage was reserved for moments of high drama and close combat. But repeated reading of the poem reveals no such consistency of approach. In fact there are occasions when the poem switches tense within the same passage, within the same sentence, sometimes within the same line, and if there is an underlying pattern or a good reason for such variation, it has eluded me. It is possible that here and there I have sacrificed some of the urgency and emotion of the original for the sake of a smooth read and to comply with modern grammatical expectations, but at the very outset the speaker in the poem assumes the role of narrator, inviting us to gather round and listen to a "tale," i.e., something that happened in the past, and I have continued in that storytelling mode.

I have used Larry D. Benson's (1974) transcription and annotations as a foundation text for this translation, with reference as well to critical editions by Mary Hamel (1984) and Valerie Krishna (1976). No transcription agrees entirely with another on the meaning of words and phrases, and even the total number of lines in the poem is a matter of debate. Surrounded by such dedicated scholarship and research I have not been in a position to judge the rights and wrongs of particular arguments, and on occasions, when faced with problems of interpretation, I have had to fall back on a sense of tonal consistency or simply trust my own poetic inclinations. Valerie Krishna's *New Verse Translation* (1983) and the translation by Brian Stone for Penguin Classics (1988) have been essential reading, and two other indispensable publications were *The Cambridge Companion to the Arthurian Legend* (ed. Archibald and Putter, 2009) and *Arthurian Studies ii, The Alliterative Morte Arthure* (ed. Göller, 1994). And I offer my profound thanks to Professor James Simpson of Harvard University for his insight and learning, and for his generous and tactful oversight of this translation through all of its many drafts.

So did King Arthur exist? There are no bones, no crowns, no credible documents and no archaeological evidence of any type whatsoever to say that he did, and those geographical sites across Britain that claim some connection with his birth, his life, or his death are either those of legend and fancy or tourist destinations conceived by the heritage industry or avaricious monks. True, some modern scholarship points to a set of circumstances in which Arthur might have operated as a leader in battle, not in the south or west but in the north of England between York and Hadrian's Wall, but it is little more than a vacancy that an Arthur-size figure might have occupied, or conditions in which someone like Arthur could have existed and succeeded. It makes Arthur a possibility, and even if those odds are increased to a probability, we would still need to strip away the fantasy and the anachronisms before we could even begin to consider him as a genuine inhabitant of sixth-century Britain. On the other hand, King Arthur lives on in the imagination perhaps as strongly as he ever did, and not just in literature but as a star of screen and stage and in many forms of popular culture and high art. No matter how many times he receives his death blow and is carried to Glastonbury or ferried to Avalon, Arthur remounts and rides again. It is also interesting to note how adaptable and available Arthur has been, from the first whisperings right up to the present day, flying the flag for whoever has needed or embraced him, be it the Welsh, the Celts, the Normans, the French, the British, the Cornish, or the English. In that sense, all those claims that describe Arthur as "The once and future king" have yet to be disproved.

—*Simon Armitage*

A NOTE ON THE METER OF THE
ALLITERATIVE MORTE ARTHURE

SIMON ARMITAGE'S introduction to his extraordinary transla-
tion of the *Alliterative Morte Arthure* provides all the bearings a
reader might need to start straight in on this modernized version.
For those readers who wish to understand Armitage's own metrical
choices, and for those readers who wish to hear, and to read, the original
text, a few words on the poem's meter might be useful.

Metrical practice is determined by the deeper music of a language.
In Germanic languages the tonic, or accented syllable, is usually the first
syllable of a word. In romance languages, by contrast, the tonic syllable
falls toward, or at, the end of words. Germanic poets therefore high-
light the beginning of words with the highlighting effect of alliteration.
Romance poets (e.g., French or Italian) instead highlight the end of
words, with rhyme.

In accentual poetry, one aspect of the metrical pattern is determined
by the distribution and number of accented, or stressed syllables across
the line. Medieval English poetry derived from Germanic roots is accen-
tual poetry. Accentual poetry is distinguished from syllabic poetry,
whose meter is determined by the number of syllables in the line (e.g.,
French and Italian poetry). It is also distinguished from quantitative
poetry, whose meter is determined by the pattern of long and short syl-
lables across the line (e.g., classical Latin poetry).

Alliteration determines the second aspect of the metrical pattern.
Accent is produced by the natural music of the language. Alliteration,

by contrast, is produced by art. Alliteration (from Latin *litera,* alphabetic letter) consists of the repetition of an initial consonant sound, or consonant cluster, or vowel sound, or mixture of vowel sounds, in consecutive or closely positioned words.

Anglo-Saxon is the earlier, purely Germanic form of English used in England from the time of the Germanic invasions in the fifth century until the Norman Conquest in 1066. All poetry in Anglo-Saxon is accentual and alliterative. Only after the Norman Conquest, and the impact of French, did poets writing in English begin to use rhyme as a fundamental part of their metrical practice. Anglo-Saxon poetry and metrical practice were for the most part displaced by models of continental poetic making deploying rhyme, even if English poets continued to observe accentual patterns within the line, and even if there are some very brilliant, post-Conquest examples of alliterative poetry (notably the alliterative Lawman's *Brut,* c. 1190).

From the mid-fourteenth century, however, for reasons not fully understood, an extraordinary range of accentual, alliterative poems appear. It seems likely that this body of work constitutes a revival of an older metrical tradition. Poems written or somehow located in the West of England (naturally the most conservative linguistically, given the pressure for change from the East) from the middle of the fourteenth century deploy accentual, alliterative meter in a wide range of poetic genres. To this group of texts the remarkable *Alliterative Morte Arthure* belongs. Unlike the poet of *Sir Gawain and the Green Knight,* the poet of the *Alliterative Morte Arthure* restricts himself to alliterative meter and uses no rhyme.

The line of Middle English alliterative poetry does not contain a fixed number or pattern of accents, like the classical alliterative meter of Anglo-Saxon poetry. It does, however, have a standard pattern. That standard metrical pattern consists of two half lines, each with two accented syllables. These two half lines each form a syntactic unit, and are therefore separated by a caesura, or break, allowing a very small pause in the recitation of such verse. The standard metrical pattern is xx/xy, where x signifies a stressed, alliterating, syllable; / signifies a caesura; and *y* signifies a stressed, non-alliterating syllable. The second half line is thus linked to the first by the initial alliterating, stressed syllable. Thus, for example, line two of the original text: "And the precious prayer / of His pris Moder [mother]," where "precious," "prayer," "pris," and "Moder" are all accented, but only the first three alliterate. "Precious" and "prayer" are separated from "pris" by a caesura, or small pause.

The poet of the *Alliterative Morte Arthure* frequently enriches this basic pattern. Thus the poem's very first line, for example, enriches the pattern by four alliterating, and five stressed syllables: "Now grete glorious God / through grace of Himselven," where "grete," "glorious," "God," "grace," and "selven" are all stressed, while the first four each alliterate. Other instances reveal that the poet frequently varies from either the standard or the enriched pattern exemplified in this paragraph.

This poet also has a metrical trademark, of running alliteration across many consecutive lines, in a bravura, pyrotechnic phonic display. The longest of these units is ten lines, replicated by Simon Armitage at lines 2483–92, though there are many other shorter examples.

—*James Simpson*
Harvard University

THE DEATH OF

KING

ARTHUR

MORTE ARTHURE

Hēre beginnes Morte Arthure. In Nomine Patris et
Filii et Spiritus Sancti. Amen pur Charite. Amen.

Now grȩte glorīous God　through grāce of Himselven
And the precīous prayer　of his prīs Mōder
Shēld us frǫ shāmesdeede　and sinful workes
And give us grāce tō guīe　and govern us hēre
In this wretched world,　through virtūous living
That wē may kaire til his court,　the kingdom of hȩven
When our sǫules shall part　and sunder frǫ the body
Ever tō beld and tō bīde　in bliss with Himselven;
And wisse mē tō warp out　some word at this tīme
10　That nǫther void bē ne vain　but worship til Himselven
Plȩsand and profitāble　tō the pople that them hēres.

　　Yē that lust has tō līthe　or loves for tō hēre
Of elders of ǫlde tīme　and of their awke deedes,
How they were lēle in their law　and loved God Almighty
Herkenes mē hendely　and hǫldes you stille,
And I shall tell you a tāle　that trew is and nǫble
Of the rēal renkes　of the Round Tāble
That chēf were of chevalry　and chēftains nǫble
Bǫth wary in their workes　and wīse men of armes,

THE DEATH OF KING ARTHUR

Here begins the Death of Arthur. In the name of the Father,
the Son and the Holy Spirit. Amen for Charity. Amen.

Now may God, great and glorious, by His very grace
and the precious prayers of His perfect mother,
shield us from shame and sinful deeds,
and through His grace may we guide and be governed
in this wretched world, so by virtuous ways
we may come to His court, the kingdom of heaven,
where our soul and body shall sever their bond
and abide there by Him in bliss forever;
and may words trip from my tongue at this time,
not hollow and vain but in honor of Him,
and which profit and please every person who hears them.

    You who are listeners and love to learn
of the heroes of history and their awesome adventures
who were loyal to the law and loved Almighty God,
come closer and heed me; hold yourselves quiet
and I'll tell you a tale both noble and true
of the royal ranks of the Round Table
who were champion knights and chivalrous chieftains,
both worldly wise and brave in battle,

20 Doughty in their dōings   and dredde ay shāme,
   Kind men and courtais   and couth of court thewes,
   How they wǫn with war   worshippes many,
   Slogh Lūcīus the lithere   that lǫrd was of Rōme,
   And conquered that kingrik   through craftes of armes;
   Herkenes now hiderward   and hēres this story!

      When that the King Arthur   by conquest had wonnen
   Casteles and kingdomes   and countrees many,
   And hē had covered the crown   of that kith riche
   Of all that Uter in erthe   ǫught in his tīme:
30 Argayle and Orkney   and all thēse oute-īles,
   Ireland utterly,   as Ōcēan runnes,
   Scāthel Scotland by skill   hē skiftes as him līkes
   And Wāles of war   hē wǫn at his will,
   Bǫthe Flaunders and Fraunce   free til himselven,
   Holland and Hainault   they hēld of him bǫthen,
   Burgoigne and Brabaunt   and Bretain the less,
   Guīenne and Gothland   and Greece the rich,
   Bayonne and Bourdeaux   hē belded full fair,
   Touraine and Toulouse   with towres full high,
40 Of Poitīers and Prōvence   hē was prince hǫlden;
   Of Valence and Vīenne,   of valūe sǫ nǫble,
   Of Overgne and Anjou,   thǫse erldoms rich,
   By conquest full crūel   they knew him for lǫrd
   Of Navarre and Norway   and Normandy eek
   Of Almaine, of Estriche,   and other ynow;
   Denmark hē dressed   all by drēde of himselven
   Frǫ Swynne untō Swetherwike,   with his sword keen!

      When hē thēse deedes had dōne,   hē dubbed his knightes,
   Devīsed dūcherīes and dęlt   in dīverse rewmes,
50 Māde of his cosins   kinges annointed
   In kithes there they covēt   crownes tō bęre.

20 daring in their deeds, always dreading shame,
    kind, courteous men, courtly in their manners.
    How they won in war the worship of many,
    who ripped life from wicked Lucius, the Lord of Rome
    and conquered that kingdom through the art of combat . . .
    attend with your ears as this tale is told!

       King Arthur had at length acquired by conquest
    many castles, kingdoms, and countless regions
    and recovered the crown of all those countries
    once owned by Uther in his earthly days:
30 Argyll, Orkney, and the outer isles,
    the whole of Ireland, hemmed in by the Ocean,
    malevolent Scotland to lead as he liked,
    Wales, which he took at will through warfare,
    Flanders and France, which were his for free,
    Holland and Hainault, both of which he held,
    Burgundy and Brabant and also Brittany,
    Guyenne, Gotland, and magnificent Grasse,
    Bayonne and Bordeaux where he built so beautifully
    and Touraine and Toulouse with their lofty towers.
40 They declared him Prince of Poitiers and Provence,
    of Valence and Vienne, so high in value,
    of Anjou and Auvergne, prosperous earldoms;
    after crushing conquests they saluted him as Sovereign
    of Navarre and Normandy and also Norway,
    and of Austria and Germany and umpteen others;
    Denmark he suppressed through the power of his person,
    and from Sluys to Sweden with a swish of his sword.

       When these deeds were done he dubbed his knights
    and dealt out dukedoms in different lands,
50 anointing his relatives as royal rulers
    of the countries whose crowns they coveted the most.

When hē thēse rewmes had ridden and rewled the pople,
Then rested that rēal and hēld the Round Tāble;
Sujourns that sęson tō solāce himselven
In Bretain the brǫdder, as him best līkes;
Sithen went intō Wāles with his wyes all,
Sways intō Swaldīe with his snell houndes
For tō hunt at the hartes in thǫse high landes,
In Glamorgan with glee there gladship was ever,
60 And there a citee hē set, by assent of his lǫrdes
That Caerlīon was called, with cūrīous walles,
On the rich river that runnes sǫ fair,
There hē might semble his sorte tō see when him liked.
Then after at Carlīsle a Christenmass hē hǫldes,
This ilk kidd conquerour and hēld him for lǫrd
With dūkes and douspeeres of dīverse rewmes,
Erles and erchevesques and other ynow,
Bishoppes and bachelers and bannerettes nǫble
That bowes tō his banner, busk when him līkes.
70 But on the Christenmass-day when they were all sembled,
That comlich conquerour commaundes himselven
That ilk a lǫrd sholde lenge and nǫ lęve tāke
Tō the tende day fully were tāken tō the end.
Thus on rēal array hē hēld his Round Tāble
With semblaunt and solāce and selcouthe mętes;
Was never such nǫblay in nǫ mannes tīme
Māde in mid-winter in thǫ West Marches!

But on the New-Yēre day, at the noon ēven,
As the bǫld at the bōrde was of bręd served,
80 Sǫ cǫme in sodēnly a senatour of Rōme,
With sixteen knightes in a suīte, sewand him ǫne;
Hē salūed the soveraign and the sale after
Ilk a king after king, and māde his inclīnes;

Then as ruler of those peoples in the realms he had ridden,
the rightful King rested, convened the Round Table,
and spent that season perusing his own pleasure
in the heartlands of Britain, which he liked the best,
then went west into Wales with his warring companions
and swung to the south with his swiftest hounds
to hunt down his deer through those high hills.
In Glamorgan gladness was as great as anywhere,
60   and with his lords' assent he constructed a city
of well-built walls which they called Caerleon
on the banks of the beautiful river which runs there,
where his army might assemble should he summon them to arms.

      For the Christmas season he was seated at Carlisle,
that celebrated Sovereign, asserting his majesty
over dukes and the like from distant lands,
over earls and archbishops and others of their ilk,
and bishops, and knights whether bannered or not,
who would follow his flag wherever it flew.
70   On Christmas Day, when the crowd were all gathered,
the conquering King gave his guests a command
that no lord should so much as mention leaving
until ten days of feasting were fully taken.
So in royal array the Round Table was hosted,
amid splendid entertainment and extravagant cuisine,
and in human history never was such nobleness
witnessed in midwinter in those western marches.

      But on New Year's Day, on the stroke of noon,
as bread was being brought to bold men at the table,
80   a senator of Rome appeared suddenly in their presence,
with sixteen knights standing in his shadow.
He saluted the Sovereign and those seated in hall,
inclining respectfully to king after king

Gaynor in her degree   hē grētte as him līked
And sinn again tō the gōme   hē gāve up his needes:
"Sir Lūcīus Īberīus,   the Emperour of Rōme,
Salūes thee as subjet,   under his sēle rich;
It is crēdans, Sir King,   with crūel wordes;
Trow it for nǫ troufles,   his targe is tō shew!
Now in this New-Yēres Day,   with nǫtarīes sign,
I māke thee summons in sale   tō sew for thy landes,
That on Lamass Day   there bē nǫ let founden
That thou bē rędy at Rōme   with all thy Round Tāble
Appęre in his presence   with thy prīs knightes
At prīme of the day,   in pain of your līves,
In the kidd Capitoil   before the king selven
When hē and his senatours   bēs set as them līkes,
Tō answer ǫnly   why thou occūpīes the landes
That ǫwe homāge of ǫld   til him and his elders,
Why thou has ridden and raimed   and ransound the pople
And killed down his cosins,   kinges annointed;
There shall thou give reckoning   for all thy Round Tāble,
Why thou art rebel tō Rōme   and rentes them with-hǫldes!
Yif thou thēse summons withsit, hē sendes thee thēse wordes:
Hē shall thee seek ǫver the sę,   with sixteen kinges,
Brin Bretain the brǫde   and britten thy knightes
And bring thee buxomly as a bęste   with brēthe where him līkes,
That thou ne shall route ne rest   under the hęven rich
Thǫugh thou for reddour of Rōme   run tō the erthe!
For if thou flee intō Fraunce   or Frīsland other,
Thou shall be fetched with force   and ǫverset forever!
Thy fader made fewtee   wē find in our rolles,
In the regestrē of Rōme,   whǫ-sǫ right lookes;
Withouten mǫre troufling   the tribūte wē ask
That Jūlīus Cęsar wǫn   with his gentle knightes!"

The king blushed on the berne   with his brǫde eyen,
That full brēmly for brēthe   brent as the glēdes,

and greeting Queen Guinevere as courtesy required.
Then, bowing to Arthur, he embarked on his business:
"Sir Lucius Iberius, Emperor of Rome,
salutes you as his subject, under imperial seal;
this statement is worded with stern instruction—
his sign is its truth, so treat it as no trifle.
90 Now on New Year's Day, signed by a notary,
I serve you this summons to sue for your lands,
so on Lammas Day, without detour or delay,
be ready in Rome with your Round Table
to appear in his presence with your princely knights,
just as daylight dawns, on pain of death,
in the famous Capitol, before the true King,
where he sits with his senate in the style that suits them,
to answer what he asks of you: why you occupy his lands
that owe homage of old to his ancestral elders,
100 and why you have robbed and ransacked and ransomed
and killed his kinsmen who are royal kings.
You are called to account for the actions of your company
who are rebels to Rome and default on its revenues.
If this summons is snubbed, he sends you this warning:
he shall seek you overseas with sixteen kings
and burn Britain to oblivion and obliterate your knights,
and leash you like the tamest beast that ever breathed;
you shall sleep not one wink under watching skies
though you hide in a hole being hunted by Rome.
110 For if you flee into France or Friesland or farther
our forces shall fetch you and finish you forever.
We find in our records that your father paid fealty
to the registry of Rome, and rightly so.
No more trifling. You are told we seek tribute
won by Julius Caesar and the soldiers who served him."

The King fixed the foreigner with a fearsome stare,
the anger in his eyes like glowing embers.

Cast colours as the king   with crūel lātes
Looked as a līon   and on his lip bītes.
120 The Rōmanes for radness   rusht to the erthe,
For ferdness of his fāce   as they fey wēre;
Couched as kennetes   before the king selven;
Because of his countenaunce   confūsed them seemed!
Then covered up a knight   and crīed full loud:
"King, crowned of kind,   courtais and noble,
Misdō no messanger   for mensk of thyselven,
Sēnn wē are in thy manrēde   and mercy thee beseekes;
Wē lenge with Sir Lūcīus,   that lord is of Rōme,
That is the marvēloustest man   than on molde lenges;
130 It is lēlful til us   his līking til work;
Wē come at his commaundment;   have us excūsed."

    Then carpes the conquerour   crūel wordes:
"Hā! crāvand knight,   a coward thee seemes!
There is some segge in this sale,   and hē were sore grēved
Thou durst not for all Lumbardy   look on him ones!"

    "Sir," says the senatour,   "So Crīst mot mē help,
The vout of thy visāge   has wounded us all!
Thou art the lordlīest lēde   that ever I on looked.
By looking, withouten lees,   a līon thee seemes!"

140   "Thou has mē summoned," quod the king,   "and said what thee līkes.
For sāke of thy soveraign   I suffer thee the more;
Sēnn I crowned was in kith   with crisom annointed,
Was never crēatūre tō mē   that carped so large!
But I shall tāke counsēl   at kinges annointed
Of dūkes and douspeeres   and doctours noble,
Of peeres of the parlement,   prēlātes and other
Of the richest renkes   of the Round Tāble;
Thus shall I tāke avīsement   of valīant bernes.

His face became flushed with the fire of fury
till he looked like a lion, and he bit his lip.
120 And those Romans fell to the floor in fear,
appalled by his expression, expecting the end.
They cowered like pups in the presence of the King—
they seemed utterly alarmed by his looks alone.
Then one knight, from his knees, pleaded imploringly:
"Most natural of kings, courteous and noble,
for your honor's sake spare us emissaries from harm;
since power here is your privilege we appeal for mercy.
We are ruled by Sir Lucius, Lord of all Rome,
the most marvelous man in the width of the world,
130 and to do as he likes is our loyal duty.
We come at his command, so have us excused."

      Then the Sovereign spoke and his words were scathing.
"Ha! Craven knight, what a creeping coward.
If one knight standing near were annoyed in the slightest
you'd be loath for all Lombardy to look at him once."
"Sir," said the senator, "as Christ is my Savior,
the cruelty in your eyes has cut us to the core.
Of the lords I have looked on, you are the lordliest.
I speak no lie—your stare is lion-like."
140 "You have summoned me, and your statement is spoken;
for your leader's sake I shall suffer you still longer.
Since my head was anointed with holy oil
no beast ever blustered so brazenly before me.
But with holy kings I shall hold council,
and dukes and nobles and doctors of degree,
and peers of the parliament and also prelates,
and the esteemed ranks of the Round Table.
Valuable advice from the valiant I shall seek,

Work after the wit   of my wīse knightes.

150 Tō warp wordes in wāste   nǫ worship it wēre,
Ne wilfully in this wrath   tō wręken myselven.
Forthy shall thou lenge hēre   and lodge with thēse lǫrdes
This seven-night in solāce   tō sujourn your horses,
Tō see what līfe that wē lęde   in thēse lǫw landes."
For by the rēaltee of Rōme,   that richest was ever,
Hē commaundes Sir Kayous,   "Tāke keep tō thǫse lǫrdes
Tō stightel thǫ stern men   as their stāte askes,
That they bē herbered in hāste   in thǫse high chāmbres,
Sithen sittandly in sale   served thereafter,
160 That they find nǫ faute   of food tō their horses,
Nǫther wīne ne wax   ne welth in this erthe;
Spare for nǫ spīcery,   but spend what thee līkes
That there bē largess on loft   and nǫ lack founden;
If thou my worship wait,   wye, by my trewth,
Thou shall have gersoms full gręte   that gain shall thee ever!"

Now are they herbered in high   and in hǫst hǫlden,
Hāstily with hende men   within these high walles.
In chāmbers with chimpnees   they chāngen their weedes,
And sithen the chaunceller   them fetched with chevalry nǫble;
170 Soon the senatour was set   as him well seemed,
At the kinges ǫwn bōrde;   twǫ knightes him served,
Singulere, soothly,   as Arthur himselven,
Richly on the right hand   at the Round Tāble.
By ręsoun that the Rōmans   were sǫ rich hǫlden,
As of the rēalest blood   that regned in erthe.
There come in at the first course,   before the king selven,
Bǫrehevedes that were bright,   burnisht with silver
All with taught men and towen   in togges full rich,
Of sank rēal in suīte,   sixty at ǫnes;

and shall work by the wit of my wise knights.

150 Now, to waste further breath would find me unworthy,
as would reaping revenge in a frenzied rage.
You shall lodge here, therefore, with these loyal lords,
for seven nights be hosted and shall stable your horses,
and see life as we live it in these humble lands."

Respectful of Rome, which was ever the richest,
he commanded Sir Kay, "Take care of these lords,
serve them to the standards their status insists,
and make haste to house them in the choicest chambers,
then show them to the hall to be seated and served.

160 What they hope for they shall have, be it hay for their horses
or wine or wax candles or all of earth's wealth.
Spare no spices and spend without stint,
the breadth of abundance shall know no boundary.
Uphold my honor, sir, and hand on heart
you shall be wealthily rewarded, and never go without."

So they are harbored in court and hosted most highly,
welcomed warmly by the knights within those walls.
In their chambers by firelight they changed their clothes
then a chancellor escorted them with all due ceremony.

170 Soon the senator was seated, as his status demanded,
at the King's top table, with two knights in attendance,
by himself, singly, as Arthur would be served,
like royalty, from the right, at the Round Table.
For the Romans, in their reign, were regarded greatly,
and their blood was as royal as any on earth.

The first course was carried in before the King in person,
boars' heads strewn with sparkling silver
served by smartly dressed, highly skilled men
of noble descent, sixty in number.

180 Flesh flourisht of fermison,   with frumentee nǫble,
There-tō wīld tō wāle,   and winlich briddes,
Pācockes and plǫvers   in platters of gold
Pigges of pork despīne   that pastūred never;
Sithen herons in hedoyne   hęled full fair,
Gręte swannes full swīthe   in silveren chargeours,
Tartes of Turky,   tāste when them līkes;
Gumbaldes graithly,   full grācīous tō tāste;
Sēnn bǫwes of wīld bǫres   with the brawn lēched,
Bernakes and botoures   in batterd dishes,

190 Thereby braunchers in bręd,   better was never,
With brēstes of barrowes   that bright wēre tō shew;
Sēnn come there sēwes sēre   with solāce thereafter,
Ownde of azūre all ǫver   and ardaunt them seemed,
Of ilk a lēche the lowe   launched full high,
That all lēdes might līke   that looked them upon;
Then crānes and curlewes   craftily rǫsted,
Connīes in cretoyne   coloured full fair,
Fesauntes enflourished   in flāmand silver,
With darīelles endorded   and daintīes ynow;

200 Then Claret and Crēte   clergīally rennen
With condethes full cūrīous   all of clęne silver,
Osay and Algarde   and other ynow
Rhēnish wīne and Rochelle,   richer was never,
Vernāge of Venice,   virtūous, and Crēte,
In faucetes of fīne gold,   fǫnde whǫ-sǫ līkes;
The kinges cup-bōrd   was clǫsed in silver,
In gręte gobletes overgilt,   glorīous of hew;
There was a chēf butler,   a chevalēr nǫble
Sir Kayous the courtais,   that of the cup served;

210 Sixty cuppes of suīte   for the king selven,
Crafty and cūrīous,   cǫrven full fair,

180   Then came flesh that for a season had fattened on frumenty,
     plus beasts of all manner and many a grand bird,
     peacocks and plovers on golden platters,
     porcupined piglets which had never known pasture,
     herons half hidden in their own fine feathers,
     plump swans presented on silver plates,
     Turkish tartlets to tantalize the tongue,
     meat in pastry that would melt in the mouth,
     shoulder of boar, the best meat served sliced,
     bakings of bitterns and barnacle geese,
190   young hawks in bread, not easy to better,
     and belly pork that bubbled juicily on the plate.
     Then steaming stews to delight and satisfy,
     in azure sauce, so they seemed to be aflame.
     And fire appeared to flare from each slice of flesh
     that all lords who looked upon it would love.
     Then cranes and curlews cannily roasted,
     rabbit meat colored by the cream sauce it came in,
     and pheasant which flashed with silver flourishings,
     and dozens of dainty decorated pastries.

200   Then came claret and Cretan wines cunningly decanted
     through a system of pipes made of pure silver,
     wines of Alsace and Iberia and others of that ilk,
     of the Rhine and Rochelle which are reckoned the richest,
     and valued white wines from the vines of Venice
     from fine gold taps to tempt their taste buds.

     In the King's own cabinet, covered with silver,
     gilded goblets gave a golden glow;
     there was a chief steward, a chevalier of some standing,
     courteous Sir Kay who would charge the cups,
210   and the Sovereign possessed sixty, a matching set
     exquisitely crafted, intricately carved,

In ever-ilk a party pight   with precīous stǫnes,
That nǫne enpoison sholde gǫ   privily there-under
But the bright gold for brēthe   sholde brist all tō pēces,
Or else the venom sholde void   through virtūe of the stǫnes;
And the conquerour himselven,   so clęnly arrayed,
In colours of clęne gold cledde,   with his knightes,
Dressed with his dīadem   on his dēse rich,
For hē was deemed the doughtīest   that dwelled in erthe.

220   Then the conquerour kīndly   carped tō thǫse lǫrdes,
Rehēted the Rōmans   with rēal spēche:
"Sirs, bēs knightly of countenaunce   and comfortes yourselven;
Wē knǫw nǫught in this countree   of cūrīous mętes;
In thēse barrain landes   breedes nǫne other;
Forthy, withouten feining,   enforce you the mǫre
Tō feed you with such feeble   as yē before find."

    "Sir," says the senatour,   "Sǫ Crīst mot mē help,
There regned never such rēaltee   within Rōme walles!
There ne is prēlāte ne pǫpe   ne prince in this erthe
230   That hē ne might bē well payed   of these prīs mętes!"

    After their węlth they wesh   and went untō chāmber,
This ilk kidd conquerour   with knightes ynow;
Sir Gawain the worthy   Dāme Waynor hē lędes,
Sir Owghtreth on tother sīde,   of Turry was lǫrd.
Then spīces unsparely   they spended thereafter,
Malvesy and Muskadell,   thǫse marvēlous drinkes,
Raiked full rāthely   in rosset cuppes
Til all the rich on rǫw,   Rōmans and other.
But the soveraign soothly,   for solāce of himselven,
240   Assigned tō the senatour   certain lǫrdes
Tō lęde tō his leverē,   when hē his lęve askes,
With mirth and with melody   of minstralsy nǫble.

every part being studded with precious stones
so no poison could be secretly slipped inside
or the blend would blast the bright gold to bits
or the virtue of the gems would make void the venom.
The Sovereign himself was resplendently arrayed,
robed in rich gold, surrounded by his knights,
adorned in his diadem on the high dais,
being deemed the most dignified that dwelt on earth.

220   Then the conquering King spoke politely to those lords,
put the Romans at rest with his royal words:
"Sirs, be bold in your manner and brighter in your mood;
we know nothing in this country of notable cuisine,
for in this barren land of Britain no game is bred,
so force down the food without doling out false praise,
and fill up on poor fare, which you find before you."
"Sir," said the senator, "as Christ will save me,
within Rome's walls never reigned such royalty.
Any prelate or pope or prince in this world
230   would be happy to eat such an excellent meal."

    Then in order of worthiness they washed and went hallward,
the conquering King and his noble knights,
Guinevere with good Sir Gawain to one side,
and Sir Uhtred on the other, Overlord of Turin.
Then spices were served with no expense spared,
then malmsey and muscatel, both marvelous wines,
went rapidly around in ruby red cups
to each and all, be they Roman or otherwise.
Then the courteous King, since he cared to do so,
240   assigned to the senator some stalwart lords
to lead him to his chamber when he chose to leave,
among the mirth and merriment of gracious minstrelsy.

Then the conquerour tō counsēl kaires thereafter
With lǫrdes of his lēgeaunce that tō himself lǫnges
Tō the Gīauntes Towr jollily hē wendes
With justices and judges and gentle knightes.

Sir Cador of Cornwall tō the king carpes,
Laugh on him lovely with līkand lātes:
"I thank God of that thrǫ that thus us thrętes!
250 You must be trailed, I trow, but yif yē tręt better!
The lettres of Sir Lūcīus lightes mīne herte.
Wē have as losels lived many lǫng day
With delītes in this land with lǫrdshippes many
And forlitened the lōs that wē are laited.
I was abāshed, by our Lǫrd, of our best bernes,
For gręte dole of disūse of deedes of armes.
Now wākenes the war! Worshipped bē Crīst!
And wē shall win it again by wightness and strength!"

"Sir Cador," quǫd the king, "thy counsēl is nǫble;
260 But thou art a marvēlous man with thy merry wordes!
For thou countes nǫ cāse ne castes nǫ further,
But hurles forth upon hęved, as thy herte thinkes;
I moste tręte of a trews touchand thēse needes,
Talk of these tīthandes that teenes mīne herte.
Thou sees that the emperour is angerd a little;
It seemes by his sandesman that hē is sǫre grēved;
His senatour has summond mē and said what him līked,
Hethely in my hall, with heinous wordes,
In spēche despīsed mē and spared mē little;
270 I might nǫt spęke for spīte, sǫ my herte trembled!
Hē asked me tyrauntly tribūte of Rōme,
That teenfully tint was in tīme of mīne elders,
There ālīenes, in absence of all men of armes,
Coverd it of commouns, as cronīcles telles.

Then the Conqueror, in due course, went into council
with his lords and liegemen who were loyal to his cause;
to the Giant's Tower he went in good temper
with his generals and judges and just knights.
Sir Cador of Cornwall addressed the King
with a pleasing expression and warmth in his words.
"For the trouble that threatens I thank God thoroughly.
250 You'll be trapped by this treachery, unless you trick better.
This letter from Sir Lucius makes my heart laugh!
We have lived at our leisure now for many long days,
capering as we please through all points of the compass
till the fame that we fought for has frittered away.
I blush, by our lord, for our best baronage
whom we painfully disappoint by our abuse of power.
Now war has awoken—may Christ be worshipped!
May valor and vigor bring us victory again!"

"Sir Cador, your counsel is noble," said the King,
260 You're a marvelous man of merry words.
But you take no account of the case or its consequences,
simply hurling from your head what happens in your heart.
We must tease out the truths and proceed tactfully,
giving talk to this topic which troubles my heart.
You see that the Emperor is certainly angered,
from his messengers it seems he is mightily dismayed.
His senator has summoned me and spoken at will,
behaved hideously in my hall with hateful words,
slurring and slandering and sparing me no shame.
270 I could hardly answer, for my heart shook with anger.
Like a tyrant he told me to pay tribute to Rome,
so sadly conceded by our conquering forbears
when foreigners, in the absence of armed defenses,
claimed it from our commonwealth, so the chronicles say.

I have tītle tō tāke   tribūte of Rōme;
Mīne auncestres were emperours   and ǫught it themselven,
Belin and Bremin   and Bawdewyne the third;
They occūpīed the empīre   eight scǫre winters,
Ilkon eier after other,   as ǫld men telles;
280   They covered the Capitol   and cast down the walles,
Hanged of their hędesmen   by hundrethes at ǫnes;
Sēnn Constantīne, our kinsman,   conquered it after,
That eier was of Yngland   and emperour of Rōme,
Hē that conquered the cross   by craftes of armes,
That Crīst was on crūcified,   That King is of hęven.
Thus have wē evidence tō ask   the emperour the sāme,
That thus regnes at Rōme,   what right that hē claimes."

Then answerd King Aungers   tō Arthur himself:
"Thou ǫught tō bē ǫverling   ǫver all other kinges,
290   For wīsest and worthyest   and wightest of handes,
The knightlyest of counsēl   that ever crown bǫre.
I dare say for Scotland   that wē them scāthe limped;
When the Rōmans regned   they ransound our elders
And rǫde in their rīot   and ravished our wīves,
Withouten ręsoun or right   reft us our goodes;
And I shall māke my avow   devōtly tō Crīst
And tō the hǫly vernācle,   virtūous and nǫble,
Of this częte vilany   I shall bē venged ǫnes,
On yon venomous men   with valīant knightes!
300   I shall thee further of defence   fostred ynow
Twenty thousand men   within twǫ months
Of my wāge tō wend   where-sǫ thee līkes,
Tō fight with thy fǫmen   that us unfair lędes!"

Then the burlich berne   of Bretain the little
Counsēls Sir Arthur   and of him congee beseekes
Tō answer the ālīenes   with austeren wordes,

In truth, it is Rome that owes tribute to me!
For my ancestors were Emperors and owned it outright;
Belinus and Brennius and Baldwin the Third
occupied the empire for eight score winters,
each inheriting it in turn, as the old men tell.
280   They won the Capitol and sent its walls crashing,
and hanged their headmen a hundred at a time.
Then our kinsman Constantine was its next conqueror
who was heir to all England and a Roman Emperor,
and by armed combat captured the cross
on which Christ the Heavenly King was crucified;
on which evidence we ask the Emperor to explain
by what right those who reign in Rome make their claim."

        Then King Angus spoke, giving answer to Arthur.
"You ought to be overlord above every authority,
290   you are wisest and worthiest and the mightiest warrior,
and most kingly of counsel that ever wore the crown.
I speak for Scotland, and we suffered from their skirmishing;
while the Romans reigned here they ransomed our nobles
and ran riot through the regions, raping our wives,
robbing us blind without reason or right.
So I shall swear an oath to our Savior in heaven
and devoutly make a vow to the vernicle most virtuous,
that vengeance shall visit this great villainy
when my valiant knights vie with venomous men.
300   I shall find you the finest of fighting forces,
twenty thousand men within two months
to deploy as you please, paid from my pocket,
to attack those foes who would treat us without favor."

        Then the burly Baron of Brittany, a bold man,
gave opinion to Arthur, politely imploring
to answer those aliens with hard-hitting words

Tō entīce the emperour   tō tāke ǫver the mountes.
Hē said: "I māke mīne avow   verily tō Crīst,
And tō the hǫly vernācle,   that void shall I never
310   For radness of nǫ Rōman   that regnes in erthe,
But ay bē rędy in array   and at ęrest founden;
Nǫ mǫre dout the dintes   of their derf wēpens
Than the dew that is dank   when that it down falles;
Ne nǫ mǫre shoun for the swap   of their sharp swordes
Than for the fairest flowr   that on the folde growes!
I shall tō batail thee bring   of brenyed knightes
Thirty thousand by tāle,   thrifty in armes,
Within a month-day,   intō what march
That thou will soothly assign,   when thyself līkes."

320   "Ā! Ā!" says the Welsh king,   "Worshipped bē Crīst!
Now shall wē wręke full well   the wrath of our elders!
In West Wāles, īwis,   such wonders they wrǫught
That all for wandreth may weep   that on that war thinkes.
I shall have the avauntward   witterly myselven,
Til that I have vanquisht   the Vīscount of Rōme,
That wrǫught mē at Viterbō   a vilany ǫnes,
As I past in pilgrimāge   by the Pount Tremble.
Hē was in Tuskānē that tīme   and took of our knightes,
Arrest them unrightwīsly   and ransound them after.
330   I shall him sūrely ensūre   that saghtel shall wē never
Ęre wē sadly assemble   by ourselven ǫnes
And dęle dintes of dęth   with our derf wēpens!
And I shall wāge tō that war   of worshipful knightes,
Of wightest of Welshland   and of the West Marches,
Twǫ thousand in tāle,   horsed on steedes,
Of the wightest wyes   in all yon West Landes!"

Sir Ēwain fitz Urīen   then ęgerly fraines,
Was cosin to the conquerour,   corāgēous himselven:

and rile the Romans till they rode through the mountains,
saying, "Verily I make a vow to my Messiah
and the Holy Vernicle, that I shall hold hard
310   in the face of all Romans who reign in any realm,
and am rigged out ready and waiting for war,
less worried by the forceful wielding of their weapons
than by damp dew as it drifts downward,
less bothered by the swing of their sharp swords
than by fair flowers that spring from the fields.
Battle-hungry men I shall bring into the breach,
thirty thousand in total, all armed to the teeth,
in a month and no more, to march at your word,
and to deploy in any province just as you please."

320   "Ah ah!" said the Welsh King, "and worshipped be Christ!
Now the agony of our ancestors shall be answered with vengence.
In the west of Wales such atrocity they wrought
just to think of that war causes weeping and woe.
I shall have the vanguard, and have it as my own
till that rogue the Viscount of Rome is routed
who wronged me once, did me villainy at Viterbo
as I passed in pilgrimage through Pontremoli.
Being in Tuscany at the time he took my men,
arrested them without right then held them for ransom.
330   I promise him now no peaceful appeasement
till fortune finds us face to face
and we deal out our dreadful blows to the death.
From my purse I shall pay for princely knights,
the most mighty from Wales and the Western Marches,
two thousand all told, sitting tall in the saddle,
the most weapon-ready warriors in the western lands."

Sir Ewain Fitz Urien then made urgent inquiry,
a kinsman of the Conqueror and himself courageous:

"Sir, and we wiste your will   wē wǫlde work thereafter;
340   Yif this journee sholde hǫld   or bē ajourned further,
Tō rīde on yon Rōmans   and rīot their landes,
Wē wǫlde shāpe us therefore,   tō ship when you līkes."

"Cosin," quǫd the conquerour,   "Kindly thou askes
Yif my counsēl accord   tō conquer yon landes.
By the kalendes of Jūny   wē shall encounter ǫnes
With full crūel knightes,   sǫ Crīst mot mē help!
Theretō I māke mīne avow   devōtly tō Crīst
And tō the hǫly vernācle,   virtūous and nǫble;
I shall at Lamass tāke lęve   tō lenge at my large
350   In Lorraine or Lumbardy,   whether mē lēve thinkes;
Merk untō Meloine   and mīne down the walles
Bǫth of Pētersand and of Pīs   and of the Pount Tremble;
In the Vāle of Viterbō   vitail my knightes,
Sujourn there six weekes   and solāce myselven,
Send prikers tō the prīs town   and plant there my sēge
But if they proffer mē the pęęs   by prōcess of tīme."

"Certes," says Sir Ēwain,   "And I avow after,
And I that hathel may see   ever with mīne eyen
That occūpīes thīne heritāge,   the empīre of Rōme,
360   I shall aunter mē ǫnes   his ęgle tō touch
That borne is in his banner   of bright gold rich,
And rāse it from his rich men   and rīve it in sonder,
But hē bē rędily rescūed   with rīotous knightes.
I shall enforce you in the fēld   with fresh men of armes,
Fifty thousand folk   upon fair steedes,
On thy fǫmen tō founde   there thee fair thinkes,
In Fraunce or in Frīsland,   fight when thee līkes!"

"By our Lǫrd," quǫd Sir Launcelot,   "Now lightes mīne herte!
I lowe God of this love   thēse lǫrdes has avowed!

outside the keep of castles and their enclosing walls,

850 and has massacred many of the male offspring,

carrying them to his crag to pick their bones clean.

Just today he abducted the Duchess of Brittany

as she rode near to Rennes with her royal guards,

dragged her to the mountain where he makes his domain,

and will lie with that lady for as long as she lasts.

We followed from afar: we were five hundred strong,

barons and burghers and bachelors noble,

but he scaled his summit, and she screamed with such terror

in horror of that ogre . . . it will haunt me forever.

860 She was France's flower, and of all five realms

the fairest of the fair to be born by far,

judged the most genuine of jewels by just lords

from Genoa to Gironne, by Jesus in heaven.

She was kin to your Queen, as you're keenly aware,

of the highest royalty to reign on this earth.

As a proud King have pity on your people,

and avenge those victims so violated by that villain."

"Alas," said Sir Arthur, "to have lived so long!

Had word come of this, it would have worked out well.

870 The fate that befalls me is not fair but foul

now this fiend has defiled that fair lady.

France's fortune I would have forfeited for fifteen years

to have stood within a furlong and confronted that freak

as he snatched the heiress and hauled her to the hills.

I would sacrifice my own self before seeing her suffer.

So point me to the peak where he practices his torture;

I'll climb the crag and have my quarrel with that creature,

take the tyrant to task for his treason in these lands,

seek a truce until times and tidings are better."

880 "Do you see, sir, that bluff where two bonfires burn?

There he lives and lurks, go there as you like,

Upon the crest of the crāg   by a cǫld well
That enclǫses the cliff   with the clēre strandes;
There may thou find folk   fey withouten number,
Mǫ florines, in faith,   than Fraunce is in after,
And mǫre trēsure untrewly   that traitour has getten
Than in Troy was, as I trow,   that tīme that it was wonnen."

Then rōmes the rich king   for rewth of the pople,
Raikes right tō a tent   and restes nǫ lenger;
890   Hē welteres, hē wresteles,   hē wringes his handes;
There was nǫ wye of this world   that wiste what hē mēned.
Hē calles Sir Kayous   that of the cup served
And Sir Bedvere the bǫld   that bǫre his brand rich:
"Look yē after ēven-song   bē armed at rightes
On blonkes by yon buscaile,   by yon blīthe strēmes,
For I will pass in pilgrimāge   privily hēreafter,
In the tīme of souper,   when lǫrdes are served,
For tō seeken a saint   by yon salt strēmes,
In Saint Michel mount,   there mirācles are shewed."

900   After ēven-song   Sir Arthur himselven
Went tō his wardrǫpe   and warp off his weedes
Armed him in a aketoun   with orfrayes full rich;
Abǫven, on that, a jerin   of Ācres out ǫver;
Abǫven that a gesseraunt   of gentle mailes,
A jupon of Jerodīne   jāgged in shrēdes;
Hē braides on a bacenett   burnisht of silver
The best that was in Bāsel,   with bordours rich;
The crest and the coronal   enclǫsed sǫ fair
With claspes of clēre gold,   couched with stǫnes;
910   The vēsar, the aventail,   ēnamelled sǫ fair,
Void withouten vīce,   with windowes of silver;
His glōves gaylich gilt   and grāven at the hemmes
With graines and gobelets,   glorīous of hew.

to the crest of the crag by a cold well
which cascades down the cliffs with its clear streams.
You'll find there innumerable folk who are fallen,
and more florins, in faith, than France possesses,
and more stolen treasure taken by that traitor
than in all of Troy at the time it was toppled."

    Then the proud King cried out for pity of his people,
and lingered no longer, but strode to his lodgings.
890 There he writhed restlessly, wringing his hands,
and no person on this planet could imagine what he planned.
He called for Sir Kay, the bearer of his cup,
and bold Sir Bedivere, the bringer of his great sword.
"By evensong be armed to the hilt and on horseback
and meet by the bush where the brook runs brightly.
I propose to set out on a private pilgrimage
while the men are seated and being served their supper,
to seek out a saint by those salty streams
on Mont Saint-Michel, where miracles have occurred."

900   So after evensong, Sir Arthur himself
went to his wardrobe and at once undid his clothes,
then dressed in a padded doublet with gold detail,
and over that a layer of Acre leather,
and on top of that a tunic of the choicest chain mail,
then a sleeveless and scalloped surcoat of Jerodine.
On his head he pulled a helmet of highly polished silver,
Basle's very best, with vivid borders,
the crest and the coronal being beautifully enclosed
with clasps of costly gold encrusted with jewels.
910 The visor and face guard were devoid of any defects,
stunningly enameled and with silver-edged slits.
His gauntlets shone with gold and were edged at the hem
with seed pearls and stones of astounding tone.

Hē brāces a brǫde shēld   and his brand askes,
Bouned him a brown steed   and on the bente hōves;
Hē stert til his stirrup   and strīdes on loft,
Straines him stoutly   and stirres him fair,
Brǫches the bay steed   and tō the busk rīdes,
And there his knightes him keeped   full clęnlich arrayed.

920   Then they rǫde by that river   that runned sǫ swīthe,
There the rindes ǫver-ręches   with rēal boughes;
The rǫe and the reindeer   reckless there runnen,
In ranes and in rōsers   tō rīot themselven;
The frithes were flourisht   with flowres full many,
With faucons and fesauntes   of ferlich hewes;
All the fowles there flashes   that flīes with winges,
For there gāled the gouk   on grēves full loud;
With alkine gladship   they gladden themselven;
Of the nightingāle nǫtes   the noises was sweet;
930   They thrēped with the throstels   three hundreth at ǫnes!
That whate swowing of water   and singing of birds,
It might salve him of sǫre   that sound was never!

       Then ferkes this folk   and on foot lightes,
Fastenes their fair steedes   o ferrom between;
And then the king keenly   commaunded his knightes
For tō bīde with their blonkes   and boun nǫ further;
"For I will seek this saint   by myselve ǫne
And męle with this māster man   that this mount yēmes,
And sēnn shall yē offer,   either after other
940   Menskfully at Saint Michel,   full mighty with Crist."

       The king covers the crāg   with cloughes full high,
Tō the crest of the cliff   hē clīmbes on loft,
Cast up his umbrere   and keenly hē lookes,
Caught of the cǫld wind   tō comfort himselven.

He strapped on his broad shield, shouted for his bright sword,
strode to his brown steed and stood steadily on the ground
before stepping in the stirrup and swinging to the saddle,
reining him stoutly then steering him strongly,
spurring the brown steed as he sped to the bushes
where his men would meet him, mightily armed.
920 They rode by the river which ran most swiftly
where the branches overreached it beautifully from above.
Reindeer and roe bucked with reckless abandon
through rosebush and brake in a blissful riot.
The forest flourished in the flush of many flowers,
with falcons and pheasants and their colors and fantails
and the flash of all fowls that fly on the wing,
and the cuckoo sang clearly from the copses and groves;
with gladness of all kinds they glory in their gifts.
The nightingale's notes made the sweetest noise;
930 three hundred of them had their say with the thrushes,
so the sound of streams and the singing of the birds
might soothe him whose soul had only known sorrow.
The fellows dismounted and pressed forward on foot,
haltering their horses at safe intervals.
Then the King gave a keen command to his knights
to stay by their steeds and to stray no farther:
"I shall seek out this saint by myself alone,
have audience with the man who is master of this mountain,
and afterward make your offerings, one after the other,
940 to Saint Michael of this Mount, who is mighty with Christ."

    The King then clambered up the crag's steep cloughs,
climbing till he crested the brink of the cliff,
then lifted his visor and surveyed the view,
inhaling the coldness to keep himself calm.

Two fires hē findes   flāmand full high;
The fourtedẹle a furlọng   between them hē walkes;
The way by the well-strandes   hē wanderd him ọne
Tō wite of the warlaw,   where that hē lenges.
Hē ferkes tō the first fire   and ēven there hē findes
950   A wēry wọful widow   wringand her handes,
And grētand on a grāve   grisly tẹres,
New merked on molde,   sēnn mid-day it seemed.
Hē salūed that sọrrowful   with sittand wordes
And fraines after the fēnd   fairly thereafter.

Then this wọful wīfe   unwinly him greetes,
Coverd up on her knees   and clapped her handes,
Said: "Careful, careman,   thou carpes too loud!
May yon warlaw wite,   hē warrays us all!
Wēryd worth the wight ay   that thee thy wit rēved,
960   That mās thee tō waife hēre   in thēse wīld lākes!
I warn thee, for worship,   thou wilnes after sorrow!
Whider buskes thou, berne?   unblessed thou seemes!
Weenes thou tō britten him   with thy brand rich?
Were thou wighter than Wāde   or Wawain either,
Thou winnes nọ worship,   I warn thee before.
Thou sained thee unsēkerly   tō seek tō thēse mountes;
Such six were too simple   tō semble with him ọne,
For, and thou see him with sight,   thee serves nọ herte
Tō saine thee sēkerly,   sọ seemes him hūge.
970   Thou art freely and fair   and in thy first flowres,
But thou art fey, by my faith,   and that mē forthinkes!
Wēre such fifty on a fēld   or on a fair erthe,
The frēke wọlde with his fist   fell you at ọnes.
Lọ! Hēre the duchess dẹre—tōday was shō tāken—
Deep dolven and dẹde,   diked in moldes.
Hē had murthered this mīld   by mid-day were rungen,
Withouten mercy on molde,   I nọt what it ment;

He found the two fires with their fiercely burning flames
and forayed between them at a fourth of a furlong,
walked past the welling springs of water
to learn the whereabouts of that warlock's lair.
He forked to one fire, and right there he found
950   a woeful widow wringing her hands,
who was torn by grief and in tears, at a grave
dug out of the dirt as recently as midday.
He saluted that sad woman with words of sympathy,
and made careful enquiries on the subject of the creature.

    The unhappy widow welcomed him and wept,
climbed to her knees and clasped her hands,
saying, "Less sound, my sir, you speak too loudly.
If that beast hears you he'll butcher us both.
Curses on the scoundrel who stole your senses
960   and caused you to wander by these wild waters.
Honorably I tell you, it's horror that you aim for.
Why do you walk here, God-forsaken wanderer?
Do you hope to slay him with a slash of your sword?
A warrior even greater than Wade or Gawain
could win no worth here, I warn you in advance.
You've set about stalking this summit unsafely—
even six of your sort are too simple for his strength;
once you've clapped eyes on him you'll lack even the courage
to cross your heart, so hulking is that creature.
970   You seem noble and fair, in the first flush of knighthood,
but you are doomed to die, and that darkens my mood.
Were fifty such fellows to fight him in the field
the fist of that fiend would fell them as one.
Look, the dear Duchess, she was dragged here today,
lies dead and buried deep in the dust.
He murdered this mild one before midday was struck,
with no mercy in the world—it is meaningless to me.

Hē has forced her and filed   and shō is fey lęved;
Hē slew her unslēly   and slit her tō the nāvel.
980 And hēre have I baumed her   and burīed thereafter.
For bāle of the bootless,   blīthe bē I never!
Of all the frēndes shō had   there followed nǫne after
But I, her foster mōder,   of fifteen winter.
Tō ferk off this fǫrland   fǫnde shall I never,
But hēre bē founden on fēld   til I bē fey lęved."

Then answers Sir Arthur   tō that ǫld wīfe:
"I am comen frǫ the conquerour,   courtais and gentle,
As one of the hathelest   of Arthure knightes,
Messenger tō this mix,   for mendement of the pople,
990 Tō męle with this māster man   that hēre this mount yēmes,
Tō tręte with this tyraunt   for tręsure of landes
And tāke trew for a tīme,   tō better may worthe."

"Yā, thir wordes are but wāste,"   quǫd this wīfe then,
"For bǫth landes and lythes   full little by hē settes;
Of rentes ne of ręd gold   reckes hē never,
For hē will lenge out of law,   as himself thinkes,
Withouten līcense of lēde,   as lǫrd in his ǫwen.
But hē has a kirtle on,   keeped for himselven,
That was spunnen in Spain   with specīal birdes
1000 And sithen garnisht in Greece   full graithely tōgeders;
It is hīded all with hēre,   hǫlly all ǫver
And borderd with the bęrdes   of burlich kinges,
Crisped and combed   that kempes may knǫw
Īch king by his colour,   in kith there hē lenges.
Hēre the fermes hē fanges   of fifteen rewmes,
For ilke Ęstern ēven,   however that it fall,
They send it him soothly   for saught of the pople,
Sēkerly at that sęsoun   with certain knightes.
And hē has asked Arthure   all this seven winter;

He forced himself on her, defiled her, then finished her.
He slew her like a savage, slit her to the navel.
980 And here I have embalmed and buried her body;
in the wake of her hopelessness all my happiness is ended.
Of her countless friends, none followed her footsteps,
only me, her foster mother of fifteen winters.
I'll not strive to pass from this perilous promontory;
I'll be found in this field till the day of my fate."

Then Sir Arthur answered the old woman:
"I have come from the Conqueror, courteous and honorable,
as one of the hardest of Arthur's knights,
a messenger to this muck heap, bringing mercy to his people,
990 to meet with the man who has mastery of this mount,
seek a truce with the tyrant in return for treasures,
for the time being, until times are better."

"You waste your words," the woman said.
"He cares precious little for land or people,
and reckons nothing to riches and red gold,
but will live as he likes, a law unto himself,
without license or election, his very own lord.
He is mantled in a gown which was made to measure,
spun by specialist Spanish maids,
1000 then gathered together most gracefully in Greece.
It is covered all over in hair, every inch of it,
and bordered with the beards of brilliant kings,
unknotted and combed, so any knight would know
each king by his color and which country he came from.
Here he rakes in revenues from fifteen realms,
for on the eve of Easter, whenever it falls,
they pay it promptly, for the peace of their people,
have their least-afraid knights deliver it without delay.
For seven winters he awaits answer from Arthur

1010 Forthy hurdes hē hēre   tō outraye his pople
Til the Britones king   have burnisht his lippes
And sent his bẹrde tō that bọld   with his best bernes;
But thou have brọught that bẹrde   boun thee nọ further,
For it is a bootless bāle   thou biddes ọught elles,
For hē has mọre trẹsure   tō tāke when him līkes
Than ever ọught Arthur   or any of his elders.
If thou have brọught the bẹrde   hē bēs mọre blīthe
Than thou gāve him Borgoine   or Britain the mọre;
But look now, for charitee,   thou chasty thy lippes
1020 That thee nọ wordes escāpe,   whatsọ betīdes.
Look thy present bē preste   and press him but little,
For hē is at his souper;   hē will bē soon grēved.
And thou my counsēl dō,   thou dōs off thy clọthes
And kneel in thy kirtle   and call him thy lọrd.
Hē soupes all this sẹsoun   with seven knāve chīlder,
Chopped in a chargeur   of chalk-whīte silver,
With pickle and powder   of precīous spīces,
And pīment full plentēous   of Portingāle wīnes;
Three bāleful birdes   his brọches they turn,
1030 That bīdes his bedgatt,   his bidding tō work;
Such four sholde bē fey   within four houres
Ẹre his filth were filled   that his flesh yẹrnes."

"Ya, I have brọught the bẹrde,"   quọd hē, "the better mē likes;
Forthy will I boun mē   and bẹre it myselven
But, lēfe, wọlde thou lẹre mē   where that lēde lenges?
I shall alōwe thee, and I live,   Our Lọrd sọ mē help!"

"Ferk fast tō the fīre," quọd shō,   "that flāmes sọ high;
There filles that fēnd him,   fraist when thee līkes.
But thou moste seek mọre south,   sidlings a little,
1040 For hē will have scent himselvẹ   six mīle large."

1010   and will stalk this place, plaguing his people
      till the King of the British crops off his beard
      and it is borne by the bravest of his men to that beast.
      If you bring no such beard then it's best you turn tail;
      any other offer will end in agony,
      for the tally of treasure he takes as he pleases
      is higher than any held by Arthur or his elders.
      But if you have brought the beard it will bring him more bliss
      than a gift of Burgundy or Britain the Greater.
      Though in the name of mercy you should mind your mouth,
1020   so no word escapes it, or worse will ensue.
      Be prepared with your present, and don't press him too far,
      for he sits at his supper and will suddenly see red.
      If you heed my advice you will ease from your armor
      and kneel in your coat and call him your lord.
      This season he savors seven male children,
      chopped up on a salver of chalk-white silver
      with pickles and powders of precious spices
      and plentiful pourings of Portuguese wine.
      His spits are spun by three dispirited maidens
1030   who obey his bidding to avoid his bed,
      for their lives would be lost in less than four hours
      if the filthy urges of his flesh were fulfilled."

      "I have brought the beard," he said, "as is better for me,
      and am ready to rush there with it right now,
      but first, my dear, inform me where I'll find him,
      and if I live I shall laud you, so our Lord help me."

      "Where the flames of the fire are flaring," she said,
      "there he feeds he his face, to seek as you fancy.
      But steal toward him, going sideways from the south,
1040   for he can smell your scent from six miles off."

Tō the source of the reek   hē sǫught at the gainest,
Sained him sēkerly   with certain wordes,
And sīdlings of the segge   the sight had hē ręched;
How unseemly that sot sat   soupand him ǫne!
Hē lay lęnand on lǫng,   lodgand unfair,
The thee of a mans limm   lift up by the haunch;
His back and his beuschers   and his brǫde lendes
Hē bākes at the bāle-fire   and breekless him seemed;
There were rǫstes full rūde   and rewful brędes,
1050 Bernes and bęstail   brǫched tōgeders,
Cowle full crammed   of crismed chīlder,
Some as bręd brǫched   and birdes them turned.

      And then this comlich king,   because of his pople,
His herte bleedes for bāle   on bente where hē standes;
Then hē dressed on his shēld,   shuntes nǫ lenger,
Braundisht his brǫde sword   by the bright hiltes,
Raikes tōward that renk   right with a rūde will
And hīely hailses that hulk   with hautain wordes:
"Now, All-wēldand God   that worshippes us all
1060 Give thee sǫrrow and sīte,   sot, there thou ligges,
For the foulsomest frēke   that formed was ever!
Foully thou feedes thee!   The Fēnd have thy sǫul!
Hēre is cury unclęne,   carl, by my trewth,
Caff of crēatūres all,   thou cursed wretch!
Because that thou killed has   thēse crismed chīlder,
Thou has martyrs māde   and brǫught out of līfe
That hēre are brǫched on bente   and brittened with thy handes,
I shall merk thee thy meed   as thou has much served,
Through might of Saint Mīchel   that this mount yēmes!
1070 And for this fair lādy   that thou has fey lęved
And thus forced on folde   for filth of thyselven,
Dress thee now, dog-son,   the devil have thy sǫul!
For thou shall dīe this day   through dint of my handes!"

Screened by the smoke Arthur sped to the spot,
made the sign of the cross and solemnly swore,
then sidled forward till the fellow was in sight.
How disgusting he was, guzzling and gorging,
lying there lengthways, loathsome and unlordly,
with the haunch of a human thigh in his hand.
His back and his buttocks and his broad limbs
he toasted by the blaze, and his backside was bare.
Appalling and repellent pieces of flesh
1050 of beasts and our brothers were braising there together,
and a cook pot was crammed with christened children,
some spiked on a spit being spun by maidens.
That noble Sovereign; for the sake of his subjects
his heart bled with hurt on the ground where he halted.
Then he lifted up his shield and delayed no longer,
brandished his broad sword by its bright hilt,
strode straight toward him with a steely spirit
and hailed that hulk with heady words:
"Now may Almighty God, who all men worship,
1060 bring you sorrow and suffering, sot, there where you slouch,
as the foulest figure that was ever formed.
So offensive is your food, may the Fiend have your soul.
On my oath, you oaf, this is odious eating,
these carvings of all creatures. You accursed wretch:
because you have killed these christened children,
making them martyrs, and removed from life
who are cooked on your coals, made corpses at your hands,
I shall see you are assigned the vengeance you deserve
through the might of Saint Michael who is master of this mount,
1070 and for the fair lady who lies here lifeless
whom you forcibly defiled for your foul pleasure.
So steel yourself, dog's son, may the Devil take your soul,
for you shall die this day by dint of my hands."

Then glōpined the glutton   and glǫred unfair;
Hē grenned as a grayhound   with grisly tuskes;
Hē gāped, hē grǫned fast   with grouchand lātes
For grēf of the good king   that him with grame greetes.
His fax and his foretop   was filtered tōgeders
And out of his fāce fǫm   an half foot large;

1080   His front and his forhęved,   all was it ǫver
As the fell of a frosk   and frakned it seemed;
Hook-nebbed as a hawk,   and a hǫre bęrde,
And hēred tō the eyen-hǫles   with hangand browes;
Harsk as a hound-fish,   hardly whǫ-sǫ lookes,
Sǫ was the hīde of that hulk   hǫlly all ǫver;
Ęrne had hē full hūge   and ugly tō shew
With eyen full horrible   and ardaunt for sooth;
Flat-mouthed as a flūke   with flerīand lippes,
And the flesh in his fore-teeth   fouly as a bęre;

1090   His bęrde was brǫthy and blak   that til his brēste ręched;
Grassed as a mēre-swīne   with carkes full hūge
And all faltered the flesh   in his foul lippes,
Ilke wrēthe as a wolf-hęved   it wrāth out at ǫnes!
Bull-necked was that berne   and brǫde in the shoulders,
Brok-brēsted as a brawn   with bristeles full large,
Rūde armes as an ǫke   with ruskled sīdes,
Limm and leskes full lǫthen,   lēve yē for sooth;
Shovel-footed was that shalk   and shāland him seemed,
With shankes unshāpely   shovand tōgeders;

1100   Thick thees as a thurse   and thicker in the haunch,
Gręęs-grǫwen as a galt,   full grillich hē lookes!
Whǫ the lenghe of the lēde   lēly accountes,
Frǫ the fāce tō the foot   was fīve fadom lǫng!

Then stertes hē up sturdily   on twǫ stiff shankes,
And soon hē caught him a club   all of clęne īron;
Hē wǫlde have killed the king   with his keen wēpen,

The startled glutton glared gruesomely,
grinned like a greyhound with grisly fangs,
then groaned and glowered with a menacing grimace,
growling at the good King who greeted him angrily.
His mane and his fringe were filthily matted
and his face was framed in half a foot of foam.
1080 His face and forehead were flecked all over
like the features of a frog, so freckled he seemed.
He was hook beaked like a hawk, with a hoary beard,
and his eyes were overhung with hairy brows.
To whomever looked hard, as harsh as a houndfish
was the hide of that hulk, from head to heel.
His ears were huge and a hideous sight,
his eyes were horrid, abhorrent and aflame,
his smile was all sneer, like a flat-mouthed flounder,
and like a bear his fore teeth were fouled with rank flesh,
1090 and his black, bushy beard grew down to his breast.
He was bulky as a sea pig with a brawny body,
and each quivering lump of those loathsome lips
writhed and rolled with the wrath of a wolf's head.
He was broad across the back, with the neck of a bull,
badger breasted with the bristles of a boar,
had arms like oak boughs, wrinkled by age,
and the ugliest loins and limbs, believe me.
He shuffled on his shanks, being shovel footed,
and his knock-kneed legs were abnormally knuckled.
1100 He was thick in the thigh and like an ogre at the hips,
and as gross as a grease-fed pig—a gruesome sight.
He who mindfully measured that monster's dimension
from face to foot would have found it five fathoms.

Then he started up sturdily on two strong legs
and quickly copped hold of a club of pure iron
and would have killed the King cleanly with his keen weapon

But through the craft of Crīst   yet the carl failed;
The crest and the coronal,   the claspes of silver,
Clẹnly with his club   hē crashed down at ọnes!

1110   The king castes up his shēld   and covers him fair,
And with his burlich brand   a box hē him rẹches;
Full butt in the front   the fromand hē hittes
That the burnisht blāde   tō the brain runnes;
Hē feyed his fysnamīe   with his foul handes
And frappes fast at his fāce   fērsly there-after!
The king chānges his foot,   eschewes a little;
Ne had hē eschāped that chop,   chēved had ēvil;
Hē follows in fērsly   and fastenes a dint
High up on the haunch   with his hard wēpen
1120   That hē hẹled the sword   half a foot large;
The hot blood of the hulk   untō the hilt runnes;
Ēven intō the in-mẹte   the gīaunt hē hittes
Just tō the genitals   and jāgged them in sonder!

Then hē rōmed and rọred   and rūdely hē strīkes
Full ẹgerly at Arthur   and on the erthe hittes;
A sword-lenghe within the swarth   hē swappes at ọnes
That nẹr swoones the king   for swough of his dintes!
But yet the king sweperly   full swīthe hē beswenkes,
Swappes in with the sword   that it the swang bristed;
1130   Bọth the guttes and the gore   gushes out at ọnes,
That all englaimes the grass   on ground there hē standes!

Then hē castes the club   and the king hentes;
On the crest of the crāg   hē caught him in armes,
And enclọses him clẹnly   tō crushen his ribbes;
Sọ hard họldes hē that hende   that nẹr his herte bristes!
Then the bāleful birdes   bounes tō the erthe,
Kneeland and cryand   and clapped their handes:

but by Christ's intervention the vile creature failed,
though Arthur's crest and coronet and silver clasps
went crashing from his helmet with one clatter of that club.
1110 The King then cast up his shield to give cover,
and with his stately sword he stretched out and struck,
fetched him a blow of such force in the forehead
that the burnished blade bit through to his brain.
But he wiped the wound with his foul fingers
and in a flash threw a fist at the other's face;
had the King not been swift in stepping aside
that hit would have ended in a victory for evil.
Then the King countered, followed up fiercely,
caught him high on the hip with his hard weapon,
1120 sinking his sword half a foot through the skin
so the hulk's blood poured hot across the hilt;
through the bladder and bowels he drove that blow,
piercing his privates, ripping them apart.

Then he raged and roared, and with a rabid fury
he aimed for Arthur but instead hit the earth,
sundering the soil by the length of a sword,
so the Sovereign almost swooned at the swish of the club.
Yet the King worked quickly, countering cannily,
swiping with his sword so it slashed through the stomach
1130 and the guts and gore came gushing out together
till the grass on the ground was gloupy with slime.
He cast away his club and caught hold of the King,
clinched him in a bear hug on the crest of the crag,
clamped him ever closer, crushing his ribs,
holding him so hard his heart almost burst.
Then those melancholy maidens fell to the floor,
kneeling and praying and pleading for this knight:

"Crīst comfort yon knight   and keep him frǫ sǫrrow,
And let never yon fēnd   fell him o līfe!"

1140   Yet is that warlaw sǫ wight   hē welters him under;
Wrǫthly they wrīthen   and wrestle tōgeders,
Welters and wallows ǫver   within thǫse wīld buskes,
Tumbelles and turnes fast   and tęres their weedes,
Untenderly frǫ the top   they tilten tōgeders,
Whilom Arthur ǫver   and other whīle under,
Frǫ the heghe of the hill   untō the hard rock,
They feyne never ęre they fall   at the flood marches;
But Arthur with an anlace   ęgerly smītes
And hittes ever in the hulk   up tō the hiltes.
1150   The thēf at the dęd-thrǫwes   sǫ thrǫly him thringes
That three ribbes in his sīde   hē thrustes in sonder!

Then Sir Kayous the keen   untō the king stertes,
Said: "Alas! Wē are lorn!   My lǫrd is confounded,
Qver-fallen with a fēnd!   Us is foul happned!
Wē mon bē forfeited, in faith,   and flēmed forever!"

They hęve up his hawberk then   and handelles there-under
His hīde and his haunch eek   on height tō the shoulders,
His flank and his felettes   and his fair sīdes,
Bǫth his back and his brēste   and his bright armes.
1160   They were fain that they fande   nǫ flesh entāmed
And for that journee made joy,   thir gentle knightes.

"Now certes," says Sir Bedvere,   "It seemes, by my Lǫrd,
Hē seekes saintes but selden,   the sǫrer hē grippes,
That thus clēkes this corsaint   out of thir high cliffes,
Tō carry forth such a carl   at clǫse him in silver;
By Mīchel, of such a mak   I have much wonder
That ever our soveraign Lǫrd   suffers him in hęven!

"Let Christ bring him comfort and keep him from sorrow,
and defend him from the fiend who would finish his life."

1140   But the muscles of the warlock overwhelmed the Monarch,
and they writhed and wrestled riotously together,
weltering and wallowing through the wild bushes,
tumbling and toppling and tearing at clothes,
rolling from the ridge in an unruly muddle
with Arthur now over, then under, then over,
from the height of the hill to where hard rocks were heaped,
not slacking though they slugged it out along the shore.
Then Arthur did damage with the dagger he had drawn,
hammering that hulk right up to the hilt,
1150   but he throttled him so thoroughly in the throes of death
that he broke three rib bones in the royal man's breast.

     Then keen Sir Kay came quickly and cried:
"Alas, we are lost, my lord is done for,
confounded by a fiend, our fate is sealed:
we are finished and forced into flight forever."
They heaved off Arthur's hauberk and with their hands examined him,
from the haunches of his hips to the heights of his shoulders,
then his flanks and loins and his fine limbs,
then his back and breast and his bare arms,
1160   and were jubilant when they found that his flesh remained flawless,
gentle knights, made joyful by such justice.
"For certain," said Sir Bedivere, "it seems, by my Savior,
he seeks fewer saints the more strongly he seizes them,
he who carts such a corpse from above the cliff tops
and carries the creature to encase him in silver.
By Michael, at such a man I am forced to marvel,
that our Lord should allow him to enter heaven,

And all saintes bē such   that serves our Lǫrd
I shall never nǫ saint bē,   by my fader sǫul!"

1170   Then bourdes the bǫld king   at Bedvere wordes:
"This saint have I sǫught,   sǫ help mē our Lǫrd!
Forthy braid out thy brand   and brǫche him tō the herte;
Be sēker of this sergēaunt;   hē has mē sǫre grēved!
I fǫught nǫt with such a frēke   this fifteen winter;
But in the mountes of Araby   I met such another;
Hē was forcīer by fer   that had I nēre founden;
Ne had my fortūne been fair,   fey had I lēved!
Anǫn strīke off his hēved   and stāke it thereafter;
Give it to thy squīer,   for hē is well horsed,
1180   Bēre it tō Sir Howell   that is in hard bǫndes
And bid him herte him well;   his enmy is destroyed!
Sēnn bēre it tō Barflēte   and brāce it in īron
And set it on the barbican   bernes tō shew.
My brand and my brǫde shēld   upon the bente ligges,
On the crest of the crāg   there first wē encountered,
And the club there-by,   all of clēne īron,
That many Cristen has killed   in Constantīne landes;
Ferk to the fǫre-land   and fetch mē that wēpen
And let found tō our fleet   in flood there it lenges.
1190   If thou will any trēsure,   tāke what thee līkes;
Have I the kirtle and the club,   I covēt nǫught elles."

        Now they kaire to the crag,   thēse comlich knightes,
And brǫught him the brǫde shēld   and his bright wēpen,
The club and the cǫte als,   Sir Kayous himselven,
And kaires with the conquerour   the kinges tō shew.
That in covert the king hēld   clǫse tō himselven
While clēne day frǫ the cloud   clīmbed on loft.

        By that tō court was comen   clamour full hūge,
And before the comlich king   they kneeled all at ǫnes:

for if all saints who serve our Lord are the same
then by my father's soul I shall never be a saint!"

1170 The wise King replied wittily to Bedivere's words:
"I have sought out this saint, so help me my Savior;
now unsheathe your sword and skewer his heart,
and make certain of this, soldier, for he has sorely grieved me.
I have not fought such a fellow in fifteen winters,
though in the Aran Mountains I once met such a man
more fearless and forceful than any fighter by far,
who would have felled me that day had fortune been unfavorable.
Now hack off his head and impale it on a pike,
hand it to your squire with his steadfast steed,

1180 then bear it to King Howell who is brokenhearted,
and bid him to think better, now his enemy lies butchered.
Then hurry it to Barfleur and house it in iron,
and mount it on the main gate for all men to see.
My sword and strong shield are still strewn on the earth
at the crest of that crag where we first clashed,
and close by, the club which is cast in iron
that has killed so many Christians in the lands of Cotentin.
Trek to the top and retrieve the weapon,
then we go forward to our fleet which floats on the tide.

1190 Any treasure which tempts you, you are welcome to take,
I have the coat and the club, and covet nothing more."

So they climbed to the crag, those noble knights,
brought back the broad shield and shining sword,
Sir Kay carrying the coat and the club,
then accompanied the Conqueror to explain to the kings
what in secret their Sovereign had kept to himself,
while the blue sky brightened above clearing clouds.

Now a clamoring group had gathered at court,
who knelt as one before the noble King.

1200 "Welcome, our lēge lord,   too lọng has thou dwelled!
Governour under God,   graithest and nọble,
Tō whọm grāce is graunted   and given at His will,
Now thy comly come   has comforted us all!
Thou has in thy rēaltee   revenged thy pople!
Through help of thy hand   thīne enmīes are stroyed,
That has thy renkes ọver-run   and reft them their chīlder;
Was never rewm out of array   so rẹdyly relēved!"

Then the conquerour Cristenly   carpes tō his pople:
"Thankes God," quọd hē, "of this grāce   and nọ gōme elles,
1210 For it was never mans deed,   but might of Himselven
Or mirācle of his Mōder,   that mīld is til all!"

Hē summond then the shipmen   sharply thereafter,
Tō shāke forth with the shīre-men   tō shift the goodes:
"All the much trẹsure   that traitour had wonnen
Tō commouns of the countree,   clergy and other,
Look it bē dōne and dẹlt   tō my dẹre pople
That nọne plain of their part   o pain of your līves."

Hē commaunde his cosin,   with knightlich wordes,
Tō māke a kirk on that crāg,   there the corse ligges
1220 And a covent there-in,   Crīst for tō serve,
In mīnd of that martyr   that in the mount restes.

When Sir Arthur the king   had killed the gīaunt,
Then blīthely frọ Barflēte   hē buskes on the morn,
With his batail on brede   by thọ blīthe strẹmes;
Tōward Castel Blank   hē chēses him the way,
Through a fair champain   under chalk hilles;
The king fraistes a furth   ọver the fresh strandes,
Foundes with his fair folk   ọver as him līkes;
Forth steppes that steren   and strekes his tents
1230 On a strenghe by a strẹme,   in thọse strait landes.

1200 "Welcome, our liege lord, too long you were away.
Governor under God, great in your actions,
to whom grace is granted and given at His will,
now your presence in this place brings comfort and peace.
Through your royal right your people have revenge!
By your helping hand our enemy is destroyed,
who overran your lords and robbed them of their little ones.
No realm in disarray was so readily relieved!"
Then the Conqueror replied with Christian courtesy:
"Thank God for this grace, which He alone granted;
1210 for it was no man's deed, but the doing of our Deity,
or a miracle of His Mother who gives mercy to all."

Then speedily he summoned those shipmen in his service
to look sharp with his shire men and share out the goods.
"Take all the treasure stolen by that traitor
to commoners in the countryside, to clergy and others;
your duty is to deal it among my dear subjects,
so no person, at your peril, complains of his portion."
With kingly words he commanded his cousin
to found a church on the crag where the corpse still lay,
1220 with a convent inside where Christ could be served,
in memory of the Duchess who was martyred on the mount.

Now that Arthur the King had killed the ogre,
he went briskly in bright mood from Barfleur next morning
with his battalion about him by those beautiful brooks;
toward Castle Blank he chose the best course,
through a pretty, open plain, under chalky hills;
at each fresh torrent he found a place to ford
and with his kindly company crossed as he liked.
Then that stern Sovereign set up his tents,
1230 formed a stronghold by a stream on a stretch of land.

Anon after mid-day,   in the mete-whīle,
There comes two messengers   of tho fer marches,
Fro the Marshal of Fraunce,   and menskfully him greetes,
Besought him of succour   and said him thēse wordes:
"Sir, thy Marshal, thy minister,   thy mercy beseekes,
Of thy mikel magistee,   for mendment of thy pople,
Of these marches-men   that thus are miscarrīed
And thus marred among   maugree their eyen;
I witter thee the Emperour   is enterd intō Fraunce
1240   With hostes of enmīes,   horrible and hūge;
Brinnes in Burgoine   thy burges so rich,
And brittenes thy baronāge   that beldes there-in;
Hē encroches keenly   by craftes of armes
Countrees and casteles   that tō thy crown longes,
Confoundes thy commouns,   clergy and other;
But thou comfort them, Sir King,   cover shall they never!
Hē felles forestes fele,   forrays thy landes,
Frithes no fraunchēs,   but frayes the pople;
Thus hē felles thy folk   and fanges their goodes;
1250   Fremedly the French tonge   fey is beleved.
Hē drawes into douce Fraunce,   as Dutch-men telles,
Dressed with his drāgons,   drēdful tō shew;
All tō dede they dight   with dintes of swordes,
Dūkes and douspeeres   that dreches there-in;
Forthy the lordes of the land,   lādīes and other,
Prayes thee for Pētere love,   the apostle of Rōme,
Sēnn thou art present in plāce,   that thou will proffer māke
Tō that perilous prince   by prōcess of tīme.
Hē ayers by yon hilles,   yon high holtes under,
1260   Hōves there with hole strenghe   of hethen knightes;
Help now for His love   That high in heven sittes
And talk tristly tō them   that thus us destroyes!"

The king biddes Sir Bois: "Busk thee belīve!
Tāke with thee Sir Berille   and Bedvere the rich,

Shortly after midday, when mealtime was done,
there arrived two messengers of those remote marches,
from the Marshal of France, who met him with good manners,
seeking his assistance and saying these words:
"Sir, your marshal and minister, through your powerful majesty,
beseeches that your mercy might save your subjects,
those men of the marches who are mired in mayhem
and suffer great strife despite strenuous defense.
Now hear that the Emperor has entered into France
1240 with hosts of our enemies, horrible and huge.
In Burgoyne he burns your cities like bonfires
and butchers your barons who live in its buildings;
with a vast force of arms violently he invades
the countries and castles which belong to your crown,
cutting down your commoners, clergy and others;
without your care, my King, they will never recover.
He fells many forests and forays through your lands,
affords no pardons and brings fear to each fellow,
slaying your subjects and seizing their possessions.
1250 To the fair tongue of France these foreigners are fatal.
He tears through tender territories, so the German folk tell,
under banners draped with dreaded dragons,
sending to the slaughter by the slash of swords
all those dukes and peers who dwell in that place.
So the lords of the land and their ladies beg you,
for the love of Peter, the apostle of Rome,
since you camp in this country, to engage in combat
with that terrorizing tyrant, before time runs out.
He inhabits those hills beneath the high forest
1260 with a huge host of heathen knights.
Help us, for His love, who resides in highest heaven,
and speak boldly to those who bring us to oblivion."

The King bade bold Sir Boice, "Go, briskly!
Take Sir Berill with you and Sir Bedivere the brave,

Sir Gawain and Sir Grime,   thēse galīard knightes,
And graith you tō yon green woodes   and gǫs on thir needes;
Says tō Sir Lūcīus   too unlǫrdly hē workes
Thus litherly againes law   tǫ lęde my pople;
I let him ęre ǫught lǫng,   yif mē the līfe happen,
1270   Or many light shall lǫw   that him ǫver land followes;
Commaund him keenly   with crūel wordes
Kaire out of my kingrik   with his kidd knightes;
In cāse that hē will nǫt,   that cursed wretch,
Come for his courtaisy   and counter mē ǫnes;
Then shall wē reckon full rāthe   what right that hē claimes,
Thus to rīot this rewm   and ransoun the pople!
There shall it dęrely bē dęlt   with dintes of handes;
The Drighten at Doomesday   dęle as Him līkes!"

     Now they graith them tō gǫ,   thēse galīard knightes,
1280   All glitterand in gold,   upon gręte steedes,
Tōward the green wood,   with grounden wēpen,
Tō greet well the gręte lǫrd   that wǫlde bē grēved soon.

     Thēse hende hōves on a hill   by the holt ēves
Behēld the housing full high   of hęthen kinges;
They herde in their herberāge   hundrethes full many
Hornes of olyfantes   full highlich blǫwen;
Palaises proudly pight,   that pāled were rich
Of pall and of purpure,   with precīous stǫnes;
Pensels and pomells   of rich princes armes
1290   Pight in the plain męde   the pople tō shew.
And then the Rōmans sǫ rich   had arrayed their tentes
On rǫw by the river   under the round hilles,
The Emperour for honour   ēven in the middes,
With ęgles all over   ēnnelled sǫ fair;
And saw him and the Sowdan   and senatours many
Seek tōward a sale   with sixteen kinges

and Sir Gawain and Sir Gerin, both gallant knights,
go at a gallop to those far green woods,
giving word to Sir Lucius that his ways are unworthy,
flouting the law most foully with my folk.
I shall stop him where he stands, if I stay alive,
or many who follow him will be found fallen.
Instruct him sternly, in no uncertain terms,
to retreat from my kingdom with his notorious troops.
And in case that cursed wretch should decline,
have him come, out of courtesy, for single combat,
and we shall soon reassess the right he asserts
to make riot in this realm and ravage the people.
Dreaded blows shall deal out death,
the Lord at Doomsday shall do as he likes!"

They made ready for the ride, those noble knights,
glittering with gold upon their great steeds,
and went toward the woods with whetted weapons
to greet the grand lord who was soon to find grief.

Then those honored ones halted at the edge of a holt,
and beheld the fine housings of the heathen kings,
and heard coming from the camp a chorus of hundreds,
with herds of elephants trumpeting from their trunks.
Rich tents were erected, their walls arrayed
with silk and purple and precious stones.
Pennants and pommels of princes' coats of arms
were pitched in the valley for people to view.
The Romans themselves had arranged their rich tents
in a row by the river beneath the round hills,
with the Emperor's, with due honor, exactly at the heart,
emblazoned all over with bold-looking eagles.
And they spied him, with the Sultan and many senators,
processing through the site with sixteen kings

Syland softly in,   sweetly by themselven,
Tō soupe with that soverain   full selcouthe mętes.

Now they wend ǫver the water,   thēse worshipful knightes,
1300   Through the wood tō the wonne   there the wyes restes;
Right as they had weshen   and went tō the tāble,
Sir Wawain the worthy   unwinly hē spękes:
"The might and the majestee   that menskes us all,
That was merked and māde   through the might of Himselven,
Give you sīte in your sęte,   Sowdan and other,
That hēre are sembled in sale;   unsaught mot yē worthe!
And the false heretik   that Emperour him calles,
That occūpīes in errour   the Empīre of Rōme,
Sir Arthure heritāge,   that honourāble king,
1310   That all his auncestres ǫught   but Uter him ǫne,
That ilke cursing that Caim   caught for his brōther
Clēve on thee, cuckewald,   with crown there thou lenges,
For the unlǫrdlīest lēde   that I on looked ever!
My lǫrd marvēles him mikel,   man, by my trewth,
Why thou murtheres his men   that nǫ misse serves,
Commouns of the countree,   clergy and other,
That are nǫught coupable there-in,   ne knǫwes nǫught in armes,
Forthy the comlich king,   courtais and nǫble,
Commaundes thee keenly   tō kaire of his landes
1320   Or elles for thy knighthēde   encounter him ǫnes.
Sēnn thou covētes the crown,   let it bē declared!
I have discharged mē hēre,   challenge whǫ līkes,
Before all thy chevalry,   chēftaines and other.
Shāpe us an answer,   and shunt thou nǫ lenger,
That wē may shift at the short   and shew tō my lǫrd."

The Emperour answerd   with austeren wordes:
"Yē are with mīne enmy,   Sir Arthur himselven;
It is nǫne honour tō mē   tō outraye his knightes,

He straightened in his stirrups and strained his bridle,
went storming into battle on his stunning steed,
engaged with a giant and jagged him right through.
Then jollily that gentle knight out-jousted another,
cut a wide swathe as he scythed down warriors,
woefully wounding those who stood in his way.
He fought through the fray for a furlong's length,
felled many in the field with the force of his weapon,
and had victory in vanquishing valiant knights,
stampeding through the dale then withdrawing as he pleased.

2090

Thereafter the bold bowmen of Britain
fought with foot soldiers from foreign lands;
their well-fletched arrows flew at the foe,
piercing the fine mail as far as the feathers.
Such fighting did fearful harm to the flesh,
and arrows flashed from afar into the flanks of the steeds.
In return the Dutchmen dealt out their darts,
and their sharp missiles shattered the shields;
the bolts from their crossbows were so cruelly quick
they sliced the bodies of our brothers before they could blink.
So much did they shrink from the shooting of those shafts
that the scores of defenders on the front line scattered.
Great warhorses bucked then bounded into battle,
and in no time hundreds lay heaped on the heath.
Then hastily the high born and the heathens and others
hurdled the heads of the dead to do harm.
Those giants at the front, engendered by fiends,
enjoined with Sir Jonathal and his gentle knights,
and with hard steel clubs they clattered at helmets,
crushing down crests and crashing through brains,
slaying infantry and armored horses,
chopping down chevaliers on chalk-white chargers.
Neither steel or steed could stand against them

2100

2110

But stonays and strīkes down   that in the stale hōves,
Til the conquerour cǫme   with his keen knightes.
2120 With crūel countenaunce   hē crīed full loud:
"I wēnd nǫ Bretons wǫlde bē   bashed for sǫ little,
And for bare-legged boyes   that on the bente hōves!"

He clekes out Caliburn,   full clęnlich burnisht,
Graithes him tō Golopas,   that grēved him mǫst,
Cuttes him ēven by the knees   clęnly in sonder;
"Come down," quǫd the king,   "and carp tō thy fēres!
Thou art too high by the half,   I hēte thee in trewth!
Thou shall bē handsomer in hīe,   with the help of my Lǫrd!"
With that steelen brand   hē strǫke off his hęd.
2130 Sterenly in that stour   hē strīkes another.
Thus hē settes on seven   with his sēker knightes;
Whīles sixty were served sǫ   ne sęsed they never;
And thus at this joining   the gīauntes are destroyed,
And at that journee for-jousted   with gentle knightes.

Then the Rōmanes and the renkes   of the Round Tāble
Rewles them in array,   ręreward and other,
With wight wēpenes of war   they wrǫughten on helmes,
Rittes with rank steel   full rēal mailes
But they fit them fair,   thēse frek bernes,
2140 Fewters in freely   on feraunt steedes
Foines full felly   with flishand spęres,
Fretten off orfrayes   fast upon shēldes;
Sǫ fęlę fey is in fight   upon the fęld lęved
That ęch a furth in the firth   of ręd blood runnes.
By that swiftely on swarth   the swęt is beleved,
Swordes swangen in twǫ,   sweltand knightes
Līes wīde ǫpen welterand   on walopand steedes;
Woundes of wāle men   workand sīdes,
Fāces fetteled unfair   in feltered lockes,

as they astounded and struck at our stout defenders,
till the Conqueror came with his keen knights,
2120   and with cruel countenance cried aloud:
"I trust no Briton will be troubled by this trifle,
by bare-legged boys who have blundered into battle."
He flourished Excalibur, all flashing and flaring,
and galloped to Golapas who had grieved him the most,
and cleaved him cleanly in two at the knees:
"Come down," said the King, "and call to your comrades.
You're too high by half I have to tell you;
with our Savior's help you shall soon be handsomer!"
With his steel sword he swished off his head.
2130   Sternly in the struggle he struck another,
then set upon several with his stout knights,
and did not cease until sixty were seen off.
And so at this juncture the giants were out-jousted,
slain in the assault by steadfast knights.

Then the Romans and the ranks of the Round Table
regrouped and rearranged, rearguard and others,
and with huge war weapons they hammered helmets,
striking through strong mail with sturdy weapons.
They gave no ground, those grand warriors,
2140   then with lances stormed in on steel-gray steeds,
fighting frenziedly with flashing spears,
shearing off gold adornments which decorated the shields.
So many fighters were felled on the field
that every tributary through the trees was a torrent of red,
and swathes of green sward were swiftly bloodied.
Swords split in half, and ailing horsemen
slew about in the saddles of stampeding steeds.
Admirable men, all maimed and mauled,
filthy hair framing once-fair features,

2150   All craysed, for-trodden   with trapped steedes,
The fairest on folde   that figūred was ever,
As fer as a furlǫng,   a thousand at ones!

By then the Rōmanes wēre   rebūked at little,
Withdrawes them drērily   and dreches nǫ lenger;
Our prince with his powēr   persewes them after,
Prikes on the proudest   with his prīs knightes,
Sir Kayous, Sir Clēgis,   Sir Bedvere the rich,
Encounters them at the cliff   with clęne men of armes;
Fightes fast in the firth,   frithes nǫ wēpen,
2160   Felled at the first come   five hundreth at ǫnes!
And when they fande them for-set   with our fērs knightes,
Few men again fęlę   mot fich them better,
Fightes with all the frap,   foines with spęres,
And fǫught with the frekkest   that tō Fraunce lǫnges.
But Sir Kayous the keen   castes in fewter,
Chāses on a courser   and tō a king rīdes;
With a launce of Lettow   hē thirles his sīdes
That the liver and the lunges   on the launċe lenges;
The shaft shuddered and shot   in the shīre berne,
2170   And sǫught throughout the shēld   and in the shalk restes.
But Kayous at the in-come   was keeped unfair
With a coward knight   of the kith rich;
At the turning that tīme   the traitour him hit
In through the felettes   and in the flank after
That the bustous launce   the bewelles entāmed,
That braste at the brawling   and brǫke in the middes.
Sir Kayous knew well   by that kidd wound
That hē was dęde of the dint   and dōne out of līfe;
Then hē raikes in array   and on rǫw rīdes,
2180   On this rēal renk   his dęde tō revenge:
"Keep thee, coward!"   and calles him soon,
Clēves him with his clēre brand   clęnlich in sonder:

2150   were trodden and trampled by horses in their trappings,
the fairest on earth that were ever formed;
for as far as a furlong a thousand lay felled.

    By now the Romans were reeling rather,
and in dread delayed no longer in withdrawing.
Our powerful prince pursued them promptly,
pouncing on their proudest with impressive knights:
Sir Kay, Sir Clegis, and Sir Cleremond the noble
encountered them at the cliff with accomplished fighters,
sparred wildly in the woods, sparing no weapon,
2160   felling fully five hundred in the first attack.
And when their troops noticed how our knights had trapped them,
despite being fewer, they were forced to regroup,
and barged into battle, brandishing their spears,
clashing with France's foremost fighters.
Then keen Sir Kay made ready and rode,
went challenging on his charger to chase down a king,
and landed his lance from Lithuania in his side
so that spleen and lungs were skewered on the spear;
with a shudder the shaft pierced the shining knight,
2170   shooting through his shield, shoving through his body.
But as Kay drove forward, he was caught unfairly
by a lily-livered knight of royal lands;
as he tried to turn the traitor hit him,
first in the loins, then farther through the flank;
the brutal lance buried into his bowels,
burst them in the brawl, then broke in the middle.
Sir Kay knew well from that cruel wound
that the dint was his undoing and death would follow.
Then he rallied himself and rode at their ranks,
2180   advancing on that villain in search of vengeance.
"Take care, coward," he called toward him,
then cleaved him cleanly, sundered him with his sword.

"Had thou well delt   thy dint with thy handes,
I had forgiven thee my dede,   by Crīst now of heven!"

He wendes tō the wīse king   and winly him greetes:
"I am wāthely wounded,   waresh mon I never;
Work now thy worship,   as the world askes.
And bring mē tō burīal;   bid I no more.
Greet well my lādy the queen,   yif thee world happen,
2190   And all the burlich birdes   that tō her bowr longes;
And my worthily wīfe,   that wrathed mē never,
Bid her for her worship   work for my soul!"

The kinges confessour come   with Crīst in his handes,
For tō comfort the knight,   kend him the wordes;
The knight covered on his knees   with a kaunt herte,
And caught his Crēatour   that comfortes us all.
Then rōmes the rich king   for rewth at his herte,
Rīdes intō the rout   his dede tō revenge,
Pressed intō the plump   and with a prince meetes
2200   That was eier of Egypt   in those este marches,
Clēves him with Caliburn   clenlich in sonder!
He broches ēven through the berne   and the saddle bristes,
And at the back of the blonk   the bewelles entāmed!
Manly in his malencoly   hē meetes another;
The middle of that mighty   that him much grēved
Hē merkes through the mailes   the middes in sonder,
That the middes of the man   on the mount falles,
The tother half of the haunch   on the horse leved;
Of that hurt, as I hope,   heles hē never!
2210   He shot through the sheltrons   with his sharp wēpen,
Shalkes hē shrede through   and shrinked mailes;
Banners hē bore down,   brittened shēldes;
Brothely with brown steel   his brēthe hē there wrekes;
Wrothely hē wrīthes   by wightness of strenghe,

"Had my deathblow been dealt with an honest hand,
then by God in heaven, I would grant you forgiveness."

He went to his wise King and greeted him worthily:
"I am grievously wounded and my grave awaits.
Work at your duty as the world would wish it
and bring me to burial—I bid nothing more.
Greet my lady Queen, if luck allows your life,
2190 and those beauteous ladies belonging to her bower.
And my worthy wife, who never wronged me,
implore her to plead for my soul in her prayers."

The King's confessor came with Christ in his hands
to console the knight and absolve him of sin.
And with a noble heart the knight knelt,
to receive his Creator, who comforts us all.
Then the King howled with great hurt in his heart,
and rode into the rout to wreak his revenge.
He ploughed through the pack, and met with a prince
2200 who was heir of Egypt in those eastern marches,
and with Excalibur clinically cleaved him in half,
sliced that soldier, even split the saddle,
so the steed's back was strewn with his bowels.
Savage in his sorrow he sought out another:
through the abdomen of one who had angered him hugely
he tilted and tore him in two through his mail,
so half of that hostile lay heaped on the earth
and the other half rode onward still seated on his horse.
From that hurt, I assume, he will struggle to heal!
2210 Wielding his weapon he wiped out defenders,
shredding men in their shimmering suits,
bringing down banners and obliterating shields,
brutal in his rage with his burnished blade.
Wrathfully he writhed and by force of will

Woundes thēse widerwinnes,   warrayed knightes
Thrēped through the thickes   thirteen sīthes,
Thringes thrǫly in the throng   and thriches ēven after!

Then Sir Gawain the good   with worshipful knightes
Wendes in the avauntward   by thǫ wood hemmes,
Was ware of Sir Lūcīus   on land there hē hōves
With lǫrdes and lēge-men   that tō himself lǫnged.
Then the Emperour enkerly   askes him soon:
"What will thou, Wawain?   Work for thy wēpen?
I wǫt by thy wāvering   thou wilnes after sorrow;
I shall bē wroken on thee, wretch,   for all thy gręte wordes!"

Hē laght out a lǫng sword   and lūshed on fast,
And Sir Līonel in the land   lǫrdly him strīkes,
Hittes him on the hęd   that the helm bristes,
Hurtes his herne-pan   an hand-brēd large!
Thus hē layes on the lump   and lǫrdly them served,
Wounded worthily   worshipful knightes,
Fightes with Florent,   that best is of swordes,
Til the fǫmand blood   til his fist runnes!

Then the Rōmans relēved   that ęre were rebūked,
And all tōrattes our men   with their reste horses;
For they see their chēftain   bē chauffed so sǫre,
They chāse and chop down   our chevalrous knightes!
Sir Bedvere was borne through   and his brēste thirled
With a burlich brand,   brǫde at the hiltes;
The rēal rank steel   tō his herte runnes,
And hē rushes tō the erthe;   rewth is the mǫre!

Then the conquerour took keep   and cǫme with his strenghes
Tō rescūe the rich men   of the Round Tāble,
Tō outraye the Emperour,   yif aunter it shew,

he assaulted soldiers and assailed knights,
went thrashing in the thick of it thirteen times,
pressed hard in the throng and thrust straight through.

    Then good Sir Gawain with gracious knights
advanced in the vanguard by the verge of the wood,
2220 and as he looked saw Sir Lucius lying in wait
with lords and liegemen loyal to his cause.
Then eagerly the Emperor quickly asked:
"Are you wanting work for your weapon, Gawain?
I sense from your unease that you seek out sorrow.
I shall wreck you, you wretch, for the boldness of your bragging."
He unleashed a long sword and lashed out swiftly,
lunging at Sir Lionel and with a lusty blow
hitting hard at his head, hacking open his helmet
and splitting his skull to a span's depth.
2230 Then he launched at our brothers like a born leader,
wounding our worthy and noble warriors,
fencing with Florent, the finest of our swordsmen,
till foaming blood flowed across his fist.

    Then the routed Romans revived and rallied,
scattering our ranks on their rested steeds;
cheered that their chief was so ruthless in his challenge
they chased and chopped down our chivalrous knights.
Sir Bedivere was pierced, punctured at the breast
by a huge weapon, wide at the hilt,
2240 struck through the heart by the stropped steel,
and was hurled to the earth; such heavy sorrow.

    Then the Conqueror, noticing, came countering with numbers
to rescue the royal men of the Round Table
and finish the Emperor if fortune ran fair.

Ēven tō the ęgle,   and "Arthur!" ascrīes.
The Emperour then ęgerly   at Arthur hē strīkes,
Awkward on the umbrēre,   and ęgerly him hittes;
The nāked sword at the nǫse   noyes him sǫre;
The blood of the bǫld king   ǫver the brēste runnes,
2250 Bebledde all the brǫde shēld   and the bright mailes!
Our bǫld king bowes the blonk   by the bright brīdle,
With his burlich brand   a buffet him ręches
Through the breny and brēste   with his bright wēpen;
O slant down frǫ the slot   hē slittes him at ǫnes!
Thus endes the Emperour   of Arthure handes,
And all his austeren hǫst   there-of were affrayed.

Now they ferk tō the firth,   a few that are lęved,
For fęrdness of our folk,   by the fresh strandes;
The flowr of our fērs men   on feraunt steedes
2260 Followes frekly on the frēkes   that frayed was never.
Then the kidd conquerour   crīes full loud:
"Cosin of Cornwall,   tāke keep tō thyselven
That nǫ capitain bē keeped   for nǫne silver,
Ęre Sir Kayous dęde   bē crūelly venged!"

"Nay," says Sir Cador,   "sǫ mē Crīst help!
There ne is kaiser ne king   that under Crīst regnes
That I ne shall kill cǫld-dęde   by craft of my handes!"

There might men see chēftains   on chalk-whīte steedes
Chop down in the chāse   chevalry nǫble,
2270 Rōmanes the richest   and rēal kinges,
Braste with rank steel   their ribbes in sonder,
Braines forbrusten   through burnisht helmes,
With brandes forbrittened   on brǫde in the landes;
They hewed down hęthen men   with hilted swordes,
By hǫle hundrethes on hīe   by the holt ēves;

They headed for the eagle; "Arthur" they hollered.
Eagerly the Emperor lashed out at Arthur,
caught him with a cross stroke and cracked his visor;
the naked sword swung swiftly at his nose
so the blood of the King streamed brightly on his breast
2250 and ran red on his shield and shimmering armor.
Our bold King spun about with the sparkling bridle
and rode within reach to run him through,
piercing mail and man with his mighty sword,
opening him slantwise from his Adam's apple.
So ended the Emperor at Arthur's hands,
and his fellows and friends looked on afraid.

Now the few that were left went fleeing to the forest
by the fresh streams, out of fear of our folk,
and the cream of our army on iron-gray horses
2260 followed those who tasted fear for the very first time.
Then the crowned Conqueror called to his comrade:
"Cousin of Cornwall, oversee this decree:
that no captain be captured and kept for silver
till Sir Kay's vile killing is viciously avenged."

"No," cried Sir Cador, "so Christ help me.
No kaiser or king under Christ's reign
will escape cold death by the craft of my hands."

Then chieftains could be witnessed on chalk-white chargers
chasing and chopping down chivalrous chevaliers,
2270 regal Romans and royal kings,
their ribs ripped apart by ripe steel.
Brains burst through their burnished helmets,
battered by blade on those broad fields.
They hewed down heathens with hilted swords
with a host of hundreds by the edge of the holt.

There might nǫ silver them sāve   ne succour their līves,
Sowdan, ne sarazen,   ne senatour of Rōme.

Then relēves the renkes   of the Round Tāble,
By the rich river   that runnes sǫ fair;
2280 Lodges them lovely   by thǫ līthe strandes,
All on lǫwe in the land,   thǫse lǫrdlich bernes.
They kaire tō the carrīage   and took what them līkes,
Camels and cokadrisses   and coffers full rich,
Hackes and hackenays   and horses of armes,
Housing and herberāge   of hęthen kinges;
They drew out dromedarīes   of dīverse lǫrdes,
Moilles milk-whīte   and marvēlous bęstes,
Olfendes and arrabys   and olyfauntes nǫble
That are of the Orīent   with honourāble kinges.

2290 But Sir Arthur anǫn   ayeres thereafter
Ēven tō the emperour   with honourāble kinges,
Laght him up full lovelyly   with lǫrdlich knightes,
And led him tō the layer   there the king ligges.
Then harawdes hīely   at hest of the lǫrdes,
Huntes up the haythemen   that on height ligges,
The Sowdan of Surry   and certain kinges,
Sixty of the chēf   senatours of Rōme.
Then they buskes and bawmed   thir burlich kinges,
Sewed them in sendell   sixty-fǫld after,
2300 Lapped them in lęde,   less that they sholde
Chānge or chauffe   yif they might eschēve
Clǫsed in kēstes   clęne untō Rōme,
With their banners aboven,   their badges there-under,
In what countree they kaire,   that knightes might knǫw
Ęch king by his colours,   in kith where hē lenged.

Anǫn ǫn the second day,   soon by the morn,
Twǫ senatours there come   and certain knightes,

No silver could save them or secure their souls,
not sultan nor Saracen nor senator of Rome.

Then together the Round Table rallied and regrouped
by the fine river that flowed so fair,
2280   stopped and took stock by those pleasant streams,
in the flatlands by the foreshore, that courageous force.
Then they cantered to the encampment to claim what they pleased:
camels and crocodiles and crammed coffers,
hackneys and asses and armored horses,
the marquees and canopies of heathen kings.
They led away dromedaries of different lords,
and milk-white mules and many marvelous beasts,
Arab horses and imperious elephants
that issued from the Orient with lords of high office.

2290   But in the aftermath Sir Arthur went at once
with an escort of honorable allies to the Emperor,
then his lords lifted his body lovingly
and bore him to a bed in the Sovereign's own suite.
Then with haste the heralds, at their lord's behest,
went hunting for heathens lying fallen on the heath,
the Sultan of Syria and his sworn kings,
sixty of Rome's most celebrated senators.
They laid out and anointed the noble kings,
lapped them in sixty loops of choice linen
2300   then lapped them in lead, to preserve them longer
and to keep, if they could, the corpses from decaying
before arriving in Rome enclosed in a casket,
with banners above and badges below,
announcing as they went so all knights would know
each king by his colors and the country of his crown.

Subsequently on the second day soon after dawn
two senators with their manly soldiers emerged

Hoodless frọ the hẹthe,   ọver the holt-ēves,
Bare-foot over the bente   with brandes sọ rich,
2310 Bowes tō the bọld king   and biddes him the hiltes.
Whether hē will hang them or hẹdde   or họld them on life,
Kneeled before the conquerour   in kirtels alone,
With careful countenaunce   they carped thēse wordes:
"Twọ senatours wē are,   thy subjettes of Rōme,
That has sāved our līfe   by thēse salt strandes,
Hid us in the high wood   through the helping of Crīst,
Beseekes thee of succour,   as soveraign and lọrd;
Graunt us līfe and limm   with liberal herte,
For His love That thee lente   this lọrdship in erthe!"

2320   "I graunt," quọd the good king,   "through grāce of myselven;
I give you līfe and limm   and lẹve for tō pass,
Sọ yē dō my messāge   menskfully at Rōme,
That ilke charge that I you give hēre   before my chēf knightes."

    "Yes," says the senatours,   "that shall wē ensūre,
Sēkerly by our trewthes,   thy sayinges tō fulfill;
Wē shall let for nọ lēde   that lives in erthe,
For pọpe ne for potestate   ne prince sọ nọble,
That wē ne shall lēly in land   thy letteres prōnounce,
For dūke ne for douspeer,   tō dīe in the pain!"

2330   Then the bannerettes of Bretain   brọught them tō tents
There barbours were boun   with bāsins on loft;
With warm water, īwis,   they wet them full soon;
They shọven thēse shalkes   shāpely thereafter
Tō reckon thēse Rōmanes   recrēant and yēlden;
Forthy shọve they them tō shew   for skomfit of Rōme.
They coupled the kestes   on camelles belīve,
On asses and arrabyes,   thēse honourāble kinges;
The Emperour for honour   all by him ọne,

from the heath's edge, without helmet or hood,
in bare feet across the sward with their swanky swords,
2310 bowing to King Arthur and offering their hilts,
to be hanged or beheaded or hold onto their lives.
They knelt before the Conqueror in nothing but their kirtles
then sheepishly whispered these wary words:
"Two senators we are, your subjects of Rome,
who have saved our skins by these salty streams
by cowering in the copse with the help of Christ.
As our Sovereign lord we beseech your leniency:
allow us, if you will, our lives and limbs,
for His love, who loans you your lordship on this earth."

2320   "By my grace," said the good King, "I hereby grant you
your lives and limbs and permission to leave,
providing you present my proclamation to Rome,
this charge which I shall lay before my chief lords."

     "Yes," said the senators, "we shall certainly ensure
that this deed shall be done, we swear it our duty.
No fellow on earth shall defy or deflect us,
be they pope or potentate or noble prince;
on pain of death neither duke nor peer
shall delay us from relaying every letter you pronounce."

2330   The British bannerets brought them to the tents
where barbers stood by with basins at the ready.
With warm water they wetted them at once
and in suitable style they shaved them to the scalp
to mark those Romans as surrendered men,
and by showing them shorn bring shame upon Rome.
Then quickly they coupled the caskets to the camels:
the highborn went by ass and Arabian horse
and the Emperor himself lay alone and aloft,

Ēven upon an olyfaunt,   his ęgle out ǫver;
2340 Bekend them the captīves,   the king did himselven,
And all before his keen men   carped these wordes:
"Hēre are the kestes," quǫd the king,   "kaire ǫver the mountes,
Mette full of the monee   that yē have mikel yęrned,
The tax and the tribūte   of ten scǫre winteres
That was teenfully tint   in tīme of our elders;
Say tō the senatour   the citee that yēmes
That I send him the sum;   assay how him līkes!
But bid them never bē sǫ bǫld,   whīles my blood regnes
Eft for tō brawl them   for my brǫde landes,
2350 Ne tō ask tribūte ne tax   by nǫkin tītle,
But such tręsure as this,   whīles my tīme lastes."

     Now they raik tō Rōme   the rędiest wayes
Knelles in the Capitol   and commouns assembles,
Soveraignes and senatours   the citee that yēmes,
Bekend them the carriāge,   kestes and other,
Als the conquerour commaundę   with crūel wordes:
"Wē have trustily travailed   this tribūte tō fetch,
The tax and the trewage   of ten score winteres,
Of England, of Īreland   and all thir out-īles,
2360 That Arthur in the Occident   occūpīes at ǫnes.
Hē biddes you never bē sǫ bǫld   whīles his blood regnes
Tō brawl you for Bretain   ne his brǫde landes,
Ne ask him tribūte ne tax   by nǫkins tītle
But such tręsure as this   whīles his tīme lastes.
Wē have fǫughten in Fraunce   and us is foul happened,
And all our much fair folk   fey are belęved;
Eschāped there ne chevalry   ne chēftaines nǫther,
But chopped down in the chāse,   such chaunce is befallen!
Wē ręde yē store you of stǫne   and stuffen your walles;
2370 You wākens wandreth and war;   bē ware if you līkes!"

borne upon an elephant with the eagle flying over.

2340 The King assigned the coffins to the captives
then had his say to all within hearing:
"Here are your coffers to haul across the Alps,
crammed with the measure of money you so craved,
the taxes and tributes of two hundred winters
that were lost to our heart in our ancestor's era.
Say to what senator oversees the city
that I send this sum to assess as he likes.
Bid him never be so brazen while my blood rules these borders
to make an enemy of himself anywhere in this empire
2350 or to claim entitlement to tribute or tax,
or while my time lasts I shall treat him to such treasure."

So they raced to Rome by the readiest route,
swung the bells of the Capitol to summon citizens
and all the senators and monsignors belonging to that city.
They handed over their cargo, coffins and otherwise,
as the Conqueror had decreed with his cruel words.
"We have traveled on trust to bring you this tribute,
all the rents and revenues from ten score winters
from England and Ireland and the outer isles
2360 that Arthur in the Occident occupies as his own.
He forbids you such boldness, while his blood holds sway,
to come brawling for Britain and its broad acres
or claim tax or tribute or any such title,
bar for treasure like this load, while his time lasts.
We have fought him in France and foul things have happened,
the flower of our folk are feared fallen,
no chieftains or chevaliers have escaped their charges
and chance has seen them chopped down in the chase.
So stock up and stiffen your walls with stone,
2370 and beware, for you awake a wrathful war."

In the kalendes of May   this cāse is befallen;
The roy rēal renowned   with his Round Tāble
On the cǫste of Constantīne   by the clēre strandes
Has the Rōmanes rich   rebūked for ever!

When hē had foughten in Fraunce   and the fēld wonnen
And fērsely his fǫmen   felld out of līfe,
Hē bīdes for the burying   of his bǫld knightes,
That in batail with brandes   were brǫught out of līfe.
Hē burīes at Bayonne   Sir Bedvere the rich;
2380 The corse of Kayous the keen   at Came is belęved,
Covered with a crystal   clęnly all ǫver;
His fader conquered that kith   knightly with handes.
Sēnn in Burgoine he badde   tō bury mǫ knightes,
Sir Berade and Bawdwyne,   Sir Bedvere the rich,
Good Sir Cador at Came,   as his kīnd askes.

Then Sir Arthur anǫn   in Auguste thereafter,
Enteres tō Almaine   with hǫstes arrayed,
Lenges at Lusheburgh   tō lēchen his knightes,
With his lēle lēge-men   as lǫrd in his ǫwen;
2390 And on Cristofer day   a counsēl hē hǫldes
With kinges and kaisers,   clerkes and other,
Commaundes them keenly   tō cast all their wittes
How hē may conquer by craft   the kith that hē claimes;
But the conquerour keen,   courtais and nǫble,
Carpes in the counsēl   thēse knightly wordes:
"Hēre is a knight in these clēves,   enclǫsed with hilles,
That I have covēt tō knǫw   because of his wordes,
That is of Lorraine the lēge,   I keep nǫt tō laine.
The lǫrdship is lovely,   as lēdes mē telles;
2400 I will that dūchy devīse   and dęle as mē līkes,
And sēnn dress with the dūke,   if destainy suffer;
The renk rebel has been   untō my Round Tāble,

So on the first of the month of May it followed
that the true royal King with his Round Table
by the clear running streams on the Cotentin coast
inflicted on the Romans a final defeat.
And after fighting in France and winning the field
and fiercely sending every foeman to his fate,
he announced the burial of his bold knights
who by lance and sword were swept from life.
At Bayonne he buried Sir Bedivere the brave,
and at Caen the corpse of keen Sir Kay,
covered entirely with clear crystals,
for his father had fought and conquered that country.
Then in Burgundy he bided while more knights were buried:
Sir Berade was interred and Bishop Baldwin,
and more good men, as their status demanded.

    Then afterward, King Arthur, in early autumn
entered into Germany with his army arrayed;
in Luxembourg he lingered while the injured were healed,
the rightful lord, surrounded by his liegemen.
Then on Christopher's Day he convened a council
with kings and captains and clerks and others,
and instructed them to turn their intelligent minds
to conquering by combat that country he claimed.
Then the courteous King, courageous and noble,
declared to his council these well-chosen words:
"Enclosed by cliffs in this countryside lives a knight
whose encounter I covet on account of his fame:
the Lord of Lorraine—I shall let it be known.
And they say that the acres he owns are most handsome.
I shall divide and dole out that duchy as I please
and deal with the Duke as destiny allows.
That traitor has been rebel to my Round Table,

Rędy ay with Rōmanes   at rīot my landes.
Wē shall reckon full rāthę,   if ręsoun sǫ happen,
Whǫ has right tō that rent,   by rich God of hęven!
Then will I by Lumbardy,   līkand tō shew,
Set law in the land   that last shall ever,
The tyrauntes of Tuskān   tempest a little,
Talk with the temporal,   whīles my tīme lastes;
2410   I give my protection   tō all the pǫpe landes,
My rich pensel of pęęs   my pople tō shew.
It is a folly tō offend   our fader under God
Other Pēter or Paul,   thǫ postles of Rōme;
If wē spare the spiritūal   wē speed but the better;
Whīles wē have for tō spęke,   spill shall it never!"

    Now they speed at the spurres   withouten spēche mǫre,
Tō the march of Meyes,   thēse manlich knightes,
That is in Lorraine alōsed   as London is hēre,
Citee of that seinour   that soveraign is hǫlden.
2420   The king ferkes forth   on a fair steed
With Ferrer and Ferawnte   and other four knightes;
About the citee thǫ seven   they sǫught at the next,
Tō seek them a sēker plāce   tō set with engines.
Then they bended in burgh   bǫwes of vīse,
Bekers at the bǫld king   with bustous lātes,
Allblawsters at Arthur   ęgerly shootes
For tō hurt him or his horse   with that hard wēpen.
The king shunt for nǫ shot   ne nǫ shēld askes,
But shews him sharply   in his sheen weedes,
2430   Lenges all at leisere   and lookes on the walles
Where they were lǫwest   the lēdes tō assail.

    "Sir," said Sir Ferrer,   "a folly thou workes,
Thus nāked in thy nǫblay   tō nighe tō the walles,
Singly in thy surcǫte   this citee tō ręche

always running riot with Romans through my lands.
Readily we shall reckon, if reason has its day,
who has right to those rents and revenues, by Christ!
Then we leave for Lombardy, lovely to the eye,
where I shall lay down laws that will last forever,
and take on those truculent Tuscan tyrants
and make treaties with their lay lords, which shall last out my time.
2410 I shall lend protection to all the pope's lands
and display to everyone my pennant of peace.
It is folly to offend our Father under God,
or Peter or Paul, those apostles of Rome.
If we follow our faith we fare all the better;
while I have power to pray, our Church is not imperilled."

      Without further speech they spurred on at speed,
those manly knights, to the marches of Metz,
the city where that sovereign lord held sway,
which was as lauded in Lorraine as London is here.
2420 The King forged forward on his fine steed
with Ferrar and Ferraunt and four other knights;
the seven of them circled the city walls
seeking the best site to set up their siege engines.
Those barricaded within bent back their bows,
and with fearsome faces let fly at our King,
arbalesters aiming their arrows at bold Arthur
to hurt him or his horse with their heinous weapons.
But the King shrugged off those shafts, wouldn't call for a shield,
showed himself, unshrinking, in his shining gear,
2430 lingering and at ease, looking at his leisure
over the wall to where those warriors might be weakest.

      "Sir," said Ferrar, "you flirt with folly
in nearing those walls so noticeably noble,
coming singly to the city suited only in a surcoat;

And shew thee within   there tō shend us all;
Hīe us hāstily hēnne   or wē mon foul happen,
For hit they thee or thy horse,   it harmes for ever!"

"If thou bē rade," quǫd the king,   "I rẹde thee rīde ūtter,
Less that they rew thee   with their round wēpen.
2440   Thou art but a fauntekein,   nǫ ferly mē thinkes!
Thou will bē flayed for a fly   that on thy flesh lightes!
I am nǫthing aghast,   sǫ mē God help!
Thǫugh such gadlinges bē grēved,   it grēves mē but little;
They win nǫ worship of mē,   but wāstes their tackle;
They shall want ẹre I wend,   I wāgen mine hẹved!
Shall never harlot have happe,   through help of my Lǫrd,
Tō kill a crownd king   with crisom annointed!"

Then come the herbarīours,   harāgēous knightes,
The hǫle batailes on hīe   harraunt thereafter,
2450   And our forrēours fērs   upon fẹle halfes
Come flyand before   on feraunt steedes,
Ferkand in array,   thir rēal knightes,
The renkes renowned   of the Round Tāble!
All the frek men of Fraunce   followed thereafter,
Fair fitted on front   and on the fēld hōves.
Then the shalkes sharply   shiftes their horses,
Tō shewen them seemly   in their sheen weedes;
Buskes in batail   with banners displayed,
With brǫde shēldes enbrāced   and burlich helmes,
2460   With penouns and pensells   of ilke prince armes,
Apparēlled with perry   and precīous stǫnes;
The launces with loraines   and lēmand shēldes,
Lightenand as the levening   and lēmand all over;
Then the prīs men prikes   and prōves their horses,
Satilles to the citee   upon sēre halves;
Ensẹrches the suburbes   sadly thereafter,

such an exhibition might heap harm on us all.
Let's make haste from here before some horror happens,
for if they hit you or your horse we are harmed forever."

    "If you worry," said the royal one, "then ride at the rear,
lest they waste you at once with their unwelcome weapons.
2440   It's all that I expected: you are but an infant,
and would be frightened by a fly if it landed on your flesh.
I feel no fear, may God be my friend.
If such groundlings are aggrieved I grimace but little;
they fritter their arrows by firing at my fame.
They shall want for weaponry, on that I wager my head.
My Lord would not allow any knave to have luck
in killing a crowned king with chrism anointed."

    First a vanguard of violent knights made their visit
with army battalions hollering behind,
2450   and fierce foragers, fighting on all fronts,
came storming in on their steel-gray steeds,
riding in array, the reliable allies
of the renowned ranks of the Round Table.
All the faithful men of France followed afterward,
their front lines well equipped as they flocked toward the field.
Then knights maneuvered their mounts to formation
to show off the sheen of their shining apparel,
arranged for battle with banners raised,
shouldering their shields, their helmets shimmering,
2460   pennons and pennants of princes' arms
studded with pearls and precious stones;
light-flashing lances and glittering gear
glared and gleamed and glinted to all sides.
Those superior riders spurred on their steeds,
descended on the city from several sides,
and swiftly they swept the surrounding suburbs,

Discoveres of shot-men   and skirmish a little,
Scāres their skotifers   and their scout-watches
Brittenes their barrērs   with their bright wēpens,
2470 Bẹtte down a barbican   and the bridge winnes;
Ne had the garnison been good   at the grẹte gātes,
They had won that wonne   by their ọwen strenghe!

Then with-drawes our men   and dresses them better,
For drēde of the draw-bridge   dashed in sonder;
Hīes tō the herberāge   there the king hōves
With his batail on high,   horsed on steedes.
Then was the prince purveyed   and their plāces nomen,
Pight pavil;ouns of pall   and plantes in sēge.
Then lenge they lọrdly   as them lēf thọught,
2480 Watches in ilkẹ ward,   as tō the war falles,
Settes up sodēnly   certain engines.

On Sononday by the sun   has a flēthe yolden,
The king calles on Florent,   that flowr was of knightes:
"The Fraunchmen enfeebleshes;   ne ferly mē thinkes!
They are unfọnded folk   in thọ fair marches,
For them wantes the flesh   and food that them līkes.
Hēre are forestes fair   upon fẹle halves,
And thider fọmen are fled   with freelich bẹstes.
Thou shall founde tō the felle   and forray the mountes;
2490 Sir Ferawnte and Sir Floridas   shall follow thy brīdle.
Us moste with some fresh mẹte   rēfresh our pople
That are fed in the firth   with the fruit of the erthe.
There shall wend tō this vīage   Sir Gawain himselven,
Wardēn full worshipful,   and sọ him well seemes;
Sir Wicher, Sir Walter,   thēse worshipful knightes,
With all the wīsest men   of the west marches,
Sir Clēgis, Sir Claribald,   Sir Clēremond the nọble,
The Capitain of Cardiff,   clẹnlich arrayed.

bringing out the bowmen and brawling a little,
scuffling and scaring the shield men and scouts,
breaking through barricades with their bright weapons,
2470   battering the barbican and reaching the bridge;
had the garrison's great gates not held good
the city would have fallen to their unfailing force.

    Then our bold battlers pulled back and drew breath
in dread that the drawbridge might dash them to pieces.
They went then to the camp where the King waited
with his stalwart knights saddled in their steeds.
When the Sovereign was settled, sites were identified
and pavilions of silk were pitched for the siege.
There they lodged like lords, resting as they liked,
2480   watching every ward as to how the war went,
seeing their siege engines set in place.

    On Sunday, when the sun had spread through the land,
the King called to Florent, that flower among knights:
"Our Frenchmen are enfeebled, I should have guessed this would follow,
for these folk are foreigners in these far-flung fields
and long for the food and fare of their liking.
There are fine forests here to every flank,
to which our foes have fled, where beasts roam free.
Go forth to the fells and forage through the mountains,
2490   Sir Ferraunt and Sir Floridas shall follow in your footsteps.
Our men fall faint: refresh us with flesh
that feeds in the forests on the fruits of the earth.
Sir Gawain himself will join you on your journey,
that warden so worthy, as befits him so well,
and those well-honored knights Sir Wichard and Sir Walter,
with the wisest men of the western marches,
Sir Clegis, Sir Claribald, Sir Cleremond the noble,
and Cardiff's high chieftain, copiously equipped.

Go now, warn all the watch,   Gawain and other,
2500 And wendes forth on your way   withouten mo wordes."

Now ferkes tō the firth   thēse fresh men of armes,
Tō the felle so fawe,   thēse freshlich bernes,
Through hoppes and hemland,   hilles and other,
Holtes and hore woodes   with hēslin shawes,
Through morass and moss   and mountes so high,
And in the misty morning   on a mede falles,
Mowen and unmāde,   mainovred but little,
In swāthes sweppen down,   full of sweet flowres;
There unbrīdels thēse bold   and baites their horses.
2510 Tō the gryging of the day   that birdes gan sing
Whīles the sours of the sun,   that sande is of Crīst,
That solāces all sinful   that sight has in erthe.

Then wendes out the wardēn,   Sir Gawain himselven,
Als hē that wīse was and wight,   wonders tō seek;
Then was hē ware of a wye,   wonder well armed,
Baitand on a water bank   by the wood ēves,
Busked in breny   bright tō behold,
Enbrāced a brode shēld   on a blonk rich,
Withouten any berne,   but a boy one
2520 Hōves by him on a blonk   and his spere holdes.
Hē bore glessenand in gold   three grayhoundes of sāble,
With chappes and chaines   of chalk-whīte silver,
A charbocle in the chēf,   chāngand of hewes,
And a chēf aunterous,   challenge who līkes.

Sir Gawain gliftes on the gōme   with a glad will;
A grete spere from his groom   hē grippes in handes,
Girdes ēven over the streme   on a steed rich
Tō that steren in stour   on strenghe there hē hōves,
Egerly on English   "Arthur!" hē ascrīes.

Go now, warn the watchmen, Gawain and all others,
2500   and wend your way without further words."

    They went forward to the forest, those fearless men at arms,
eagerly they entered those painted uplands,
through valleys and vales toward vaulting hills,
through holts and hoar woods gray with hazel,
by marsh and mossy morass to the mountains,
to where morning mist slept on the meadow,
where scythed hay lay strewn and unstacked,
swept down in swathes among sweet flowers.
They stepped out of their stirrups and grazed their steeds
2510   as the sun ascended, and songbirds sang
to the miracle of morning, like messengers of our Deity
bringing solace to all sinners who see it on earth.

    Then worthy Sir Gawain wandered off alone,
as was his way, that seeker of wonders,
when he became aware of a well-armed warrior
grazing his warhorse between water and woods,
garbed in gear that was gleaming to the eye,
embracing a bright shield, on a beautiful horse,
with no servants at his side but a young squire
2520   saddled on a steed and carrying his spear.
On his glittering gold shield stood three sable greyhounds,
with chokers and chains in chalk-white silver,
and gilding all was a glimmering garnet:
he was a chief among chieftains, a challenge for anyone.

    Sir Gawain watched him, welcomed the sight,
then gripped hold of his great spear, grabbing it from his groom,
stampeded through the stream on his sturdy steed,
and stomped toward that knight with a show of strength,
eagerly crying out, "Arthur," in English.

2530 The tother īrously   answers him soon
On the lange of Lorraine   with a loud steven
That lēdes might listen   the lenghe of a mīle:
"Whider prikes thou, pilour,   that proffers sǫ large?
Hēre pickes thou nǫ prey,   proffer when thee līkes,
But thou in this peril   put of the better,
Thou shall bē my prisonēr   for all thy proud lātes!"

    "Sir," says Sir Gawain,   "sǫ mē God help,
Such glaverand gōmes   grēves mē but little!
But if thou graithe thy gǫre   thee will grēf happen
2540 Ęre thou gǫ of this grēve,   for all thy gręte wordes!"

    Then their launces they latchen,   thēse lǫrdlich bernes,
Laggen with lǫng spęres   on līard steedes,
Coupen at aunter   by craftes of armes
Til both the crūel spęres   brusten at ǫnes;
Through shēldes they shot   and sheered through mailes,
Bǫth sheer through shoulders   a shaft-monde large.
Thus worthily thēse wyes   wounded are bǫthen;
Ęre they wręke them of wrath   away will they never.
Then they raght in the rein   and again rīdes,
2550 Rędily these rāthe men   rushes out swordes,
Hittes on helmes   full hertilich dintes,
Hewes on hawberkes   with full hard wēpens!
Full stoutly they strīke,   thir steren knightes,
Stokes at the stomach   with steelen pointes,
Fighten and flourish   with flāmand swordes,
Til the flawes of fire   flāmes on their helmes.

    Then Sir Gawain was grēved   and grouched full sǫre;
With Galuth his good sword   grimly hē strīkes,
Clęf the knightes shēld   clęnlich in sonder.
2560 Whǫ lookes to the left sīde,   when his horse launches,

The other man angrily answered in an instant
in the language of Lorraine, and in a loud voice
that men might listen to a mile away at least.
"What do you mean, mercenary, by rushing up so manfully?
Here you'll profit no plunder, parade as you please.
Unless you battle better and beat me in combat
you shall be my prisoner, for all your proud preening."

"Sir," said Sir Gawain, "so help me God,
such mealymouth men don't bother me for a moment.
If you prepare to fight expect pain and peril
2540 before you break from this grove, for all your bluster and bleating."

Then they leveled their lances, those lordly knights,
and spurred in at full speed on their steel-gray steeds,
striking freely with all the strength they could summon
until both spear shafts shuddered and shattered;
through shields they shot and sheered through chain mail,
spiking shoulders to the depth of a span.
So in worthy engagement both warriors were wounded,
but till their anger was exhausted they would never give in.
They grabbed at their reins and rode once again,
2550 readily those swift men slashed with their swords,
hitting out at heads with hearty blows,
hewing through hauberks with their heavy weapons.
Stoutly they struck, those stern knights,
stabbing at the stomach with steel points,
fencing and flourishing with flashing blades
until flickering fire sparks fizzed from their helmets.

Then Sir Gawain was aggrieved and greatly angered.
With his good sword Galuth he struck grievously,
cleaving the knight's shield cleanly in half
2560 so who looked to the left when his horse leapt up

With the light of the sun   men might see his liver.
Then grǫnes the gōme   for grēf of his woundes,
And girdes at Sir Gawain   as hē by glentes,
And awkward ęgerly   sǫre hē him smītes;
An ālet ēnameld   hē oches in sonder,
Bristes the ręrebrāce   with the brand rich,
Carves off at the coutere   with the clęne edge
Anentis the avawmbrāce   railed with silver;
Through a double vestūre   of velvet rich
2570   With the venomous sword   a vein has hē touched
That voides sǫ vīolently   that all his wit chānged;
The vēsar, the aventail,   his vestūres rich
With the valiant blood   was verred all ǫver.

      Then this tyraunt tīte   turnes the brīdle,
Talkes untenderly and says: "Thou art touched!
Us bus have a blood-band   ęre thy blee chānge!
For all the barbours of Bretain   shall not thy blood staunch,
For hē that is blemist with this brǫde brande   blinne shall hē never!"

      "Yā," quǫd Sir Gawain,   "thou grēves mē but little.
2580   Thou weenes tō glōpin mē   with thy gręte wordes;
Thou trowes with thy talking   that my herte talmes;
Thou betīdes torfer   ęre thou hēnne turn
But thou tell me tīte   and tarry nǫ lenger
What may staunch this blood   that thus fast runnes."

      "Yis, I say thee soothly   and sēker thee my trewth,
Nǫ surgeon in Salerne   shall sāve thee the better,
With-thy that thou suffer mē   for sāke of thy Crīst
Tō shew shortly my shrift   and shāpe mē for mīne end,
[That I might be cristened,   with crisom annointed,
Become meek for my misdeeds,   for meed of my soul."]

Her back and her breast were emblazoned all over;
she wore a kell for her hair and a coronet to her head.
And never had such a notable complexion been known.

3260   And in her white hands she whirled a wheel about,
working it with such wonder that all else was overwhelmed.
Its circle was beset with red gold and royal stones
and arrayed all around with rubies and rich gems.
The spokes were plated with pleats of silver,
their span from the center being a spear length at least.
Set on it was a chair of chalk-white silver,
checkered with rubies of quivering colors.
And around its circumference kings were clinging on,
wearing crowns of pure gold which were cracking apart.
3270 Six of them had suddenly been slung from that seat,
everyone of them crying these words as they went:
"I shall rue without rest that I reigned on this wheel.
Such a rich and royal king never ruled upon this earth:
on my mount, with my men, I had nothing more in mind
than to ride and run riot and hold the people to ransom.
In such unseemly pursuits my days were spent,
and for those dire deeds I am damned forever."

The first, a small man, had been flung to the floor;
his loins were too lean and loathsome to look upon,
3280 his locks had grown gray and at least a yard long,
he was facially gruesome and physically deformed,
one eye shone like shimmering silver,
the other was more yellow than the yolk of an egg.
"I was lord," said that man, "of unlimited lands,
and every being alive bowed low in allegiance.
But now I have nothing, not a rag for my nakedness,
and am lost without delay—let every man believe me."

"The second sir, forsooth,   that sewed them after
Was sēkerer tō my sight   and sadder in armes;
3290   Oft hē sighed unsound   and said thēse wordes:
'On yon see have I sitten   als soveraign and lǫrd,
And lādīes mē loved   tō lap in their armes,
And now my lǫrdshippes are lost   and laid for ever!'

"The third thoroughly was thrǫ   and thick in the shoulders,
A thrǫ man tō thręt of   there thirty were gadered;
His dīadem was dropped down,   dubbed with stǫnes,
Endented all with dīamaundes   and dight for the nǫnes;
'I was dredde in my dayes,' hē said,   'in dīverse rewmes,
And now damned tō the dęde,   and dole is the mǫre!'

3300   "The fourt was a fair man   and forcy in armes,
The fairest of figūre   that formed was ever.
'I was frek in my faith,' hē said,   'whīles I on folde regned,
Fāmous in fer landes   and flowr of all kinges;
Now is my fâce defādéd   and foul is mē happened,
For I am fallen frǫ fer   and frēndles belęved.'

"The fift was a fairer man   than fęle of these other,
A forcy man and a fērs,   with fǫmand lippes;
Hē fanged fast on the feleighes   and fǫlded his armes
But yet hē failed and fell   a fifty foot large;
3310   But yet hē sprang and sprent   and spradden his armes,
And on the spęre-lenghe spēkes   hē spękes thēse wordes:
'I was in Surry a Sīre   and set by mīne ǫne
As soveraign and seinyour   of sēre kinges landes;
Now of my solāce I am   full sodēnly fallen
And for sāke of my sin   yon sęte is mē rewed.'

"The sixt had a sawter   seemlich bounden
With a surepel of silk   sēwed full fair,

The second fellow who was soon to follow suit
seemed strong to my sight and a steely man of arms,
3290   but sighed sorrowfully while speaking these words:
"On that seat I once sat as sovereign and lord,
lapped in the arms of loving ladies.
But now my laurels are lost and lie littered forever."

The third man was squat and square at the shoulders,
thirty would have thought hard before throwing him a threat!
His diadem, dotted and adorned with diamonds
and studded with stately stones, had slipped down.
"In different realms I was dreaded in my day,
but am damned to death and eternal doom."

3300   The fourth looked a fairer and forceful fighter
whose figure and features were once marvelously formed.
"I was famous, by my faith, when I ruled in foreign fields,
feted in far lands, the flower of all kings.
Now my face is faded and foulness pollutes me;
I lie fallen to the floor, friendless and alone."

The fifth looked finer than the rest of those fellows,
a lusty man, and fierce. But he foamed at the lips.
His arms he locked rigid to hang on to the rim,
but he failed and fell and plunged fifty feet.
3310   Then sprang up and sprinted, spreading his arms,
then he spluttered, sprawled among the spear-length spokes:
"I was Sir of all Syria, I alone they served,
the unassailable sovereign of several kings' lands.
Now in solace and sorrow I am suddenly cast down,
and for the sake of my sins that seat is denied me."

The sixth had a Psalter, specially bound,
with a silk cover, carefully sewn,

A harp and a hand-sling   with hard flint-stones;
What harmes hē has hent   hē hallowes full soon:
3320 'I was deemed in my dayes,' hē said,   'of deedes of armes
Ǫne of the doughtīest   that dwelled in erthe;
But I was marred on molde   in my mǫst strenghes
With this maiden sǫ mīld   that mōves us all.'

    "Twǫ kinges were clīmband   and claverand on high,
The crest of the compass   they covēt full yęrne.
"This chair of charbocle,' they said,   'wē challenge hēreafter,
As twǫ of the chēfest   chǫsen in erthe.'

    "The chīlder were chalk-whīte,   cheekes and other,
But the chair aboven   chēved they never.
3330 The furthermǫst was freely   with a front large
The fairest of fisnamy   that formed was ever,
And hē was busked in a blee   of a blew nǫble
With flourdelys of gold   flourished all ǫver;
The tother was cledde in a cǫte   all of clēne silver,
With a comlich cross   cǫrven of gold;
Four crosselettes crafty   by the cross restes
And thereby knew I the king,   that cristened him seemed.

    "Then I went tō that wlonk   and winly her greetes,
And shō said: 'Welcome, īwis,   well art thou founden;
3340 Thou ǫught tō worship my will,   and thou well couthe,
Of all the valīant men   that ever was in erthe,
For all thy worship in war   by mē has thou wonnen;
I have been frēndly, frēke,   and fremmed til other.
That thou has founden, in faith,   and fęle of thy bernes,
For I felled down Sir Frolle   with frǫward knightes;
For-thy the fruits of Fraunce   are freely thīne ǫwen.
Thou shall the chair eschēve,   I chēse thee myselven,
Before all the chēftaines   chǫsen in this erthe.'

and a harp and a handsling with hard flint stones,
and the hurt which had harmed him he howled out loud:
3320 "In my day I was deemed, by my deeds of combat,
undoubtedly the doughtiest that dwelt upon earth,
but as my strength reached its summit I was slung down the slope
by that mild-seeming maiden who moves all men."

    Two kings were climbing, clambering up the wheel,
coveting and craving the crest of that compass.
"This chair of choice rubies is our challenge now
as the two on earth most intended for the top."
Like children they were chalk white, their cheeks and all over.
But the chair above them they never achieved.
3330 The furthest looked fatherly with a firm forehead,
of the finest physique that was ever formed,
and his dress was dyed a decorous blue,
fully flourished with gilded fleur-de-lis.
His companion was clad in a coat of pure silver
with a glorious cross, carved in gold,
and four little crosses to be found by the larger one,
so the king was a Christian, I knew without question.

    Then I graciously greeted that glittering lady.
She said, "Welcome, worthily, and it is well you are here.
3340 A word to the wise—you should worship my will
more than any hero who was here on earth,
for all your worth as a warrior has been won by me.
To you I have been helpful, and hostile to others,
as you have found, in faith, and so have your fellows,
for I felled Sir Frollo and his fearsome knights,
and made the fruits of France fall freely to your hand.
That you ascend to the seat I shall see to myself,
choose you for the chair before all chieftains in the world."

"Shō lift me up lightly   with her lęne handes

3350 And set mē softly in the see,   the septer mē ręched;

Craftily with a çomb   shō kembed mīne hęved,

That the crispand krok   tō my crown raught;

Dressed on mē a dīadem   that dight was full fair,

And sēnn proffers mē a pome   pight full of fair stǫnes,

Ēnameld with azūre,   the erthe there-on depainted,

Circled with the salt sę   upon sēre halves,

In sign that I soothly   was soveraign in erthe.

"Then brǫught shō mē a brand   with full bright hiltes

And bade mē braundish the blāde: 'The brand is mīne ǫwen;

3360 Many swain with the swing   has the swęt leved,

For whīles thou swank with the sword   it swīked thee never.'

"Then raikes shō with roo   and rest when her līked,

Tō the rindes of the wood,   richer was never;

Was nǫ pomerīe sǫ pight   of princes in erthe,

Ne nǫne apparēl sǫ proud   but paradīse ǫne.

Shō bade the bowes sholde bow down   and bring tō my handes

Of the best that they bǫre   on braunches sǫ high;

Then they helded tō her hest,   all hǫlly at ǫnes,

The highest of ęch a hirst,   I hēte you forsooth.

3370 Shō bade mē frith nǫt the fruit,   but fǫnde whīles mē līked:

'Fǫnde of the finest,   thou freelich berne,

And ręche tō the rīpest   and rīot thyselven.

Rest, thou rēal roy,   for Rōme is thīne ǫwen,

And I shall rędily roll   the roo at the gainest

And ręche thee the rich wīne   in rinsed cuppes.'

"Then shō went to the well   by the wood ēves,

That all welled of wīne   and wonderlich runnes,

Caught up a cup-full   and covered it fair;

Shō bade mē dęrelich draw   and drink tō herselven;

She lifted me lightly in her ladylike hands,
3350 sat me softly in the seat and presented me with the scepter,
then with craft and care ran a comb through my hair
until my crimpled locks came curling around my crown.
Then she dressed me in a strikingly adorned diadem
and offered me an orb, studded with rare stones
and enameled with azure, depicting the earth,
surrounded on all sides by the great salt seas—
the symbol which insisted my sovereignty of the world.
Then she handed me a sword with a highly polished hilt.
"Wield this weapon of mine," said the woman,
3360 "much blood has been spilt at the bite of its blade,
and as you slash and swish it will serve you unswervingly."
Then she left at her leisure, to rest as she liked
in the furlongs of the forest flourished with foliage:
no prince on earth had ever owned such an orchard,
and paradise alone claimed plants so proud.
She bade the boughs bend and bring to my palm
the best that they bore from the highest branches,
and they heeded her orders, every one at once,
all the grove's tallest trees, I tell no untruth.
3370 All that tempting fruit she enticed me to taste.
"Noble sir, make free with these fine fruits,
reach for the ripest and revel in their richness,
and rest, royalty, for Rome is yours,
and readily I shall roll the wheel by its rim
and pour you potent wine into pristine cups."

Then she went to the well at the wood's border
which brimmed bewilderingly with bounteous wine,
and calmly she caught up a cupful and raised it,
and I drank down a toast to that duchess at her telling.

3380 And thus shō led mē about   the lenghe of an hour,
With all līking and love   that any lēde sholde.

"But at the mid-day full ēven   all her mood changed,
And māde much menāce   with marvēlous wordes.
When I crīed upon her,   shē cast down her browes:
'King, thou carpes for nǫught,   by Crīst that mē māde!
For thou shall lōse this laik   and thy līfe after;
Thou has lived in delīte   and lǫrdshippes ynow!'

"About shō whirles the wheel   and whirles mē under,
Til all my quarters that whīle   were quasht all tō pēces,
3390 And with that chair my chin   was chopped in sonder;
And I have shivered for chele   sēnn mē this chaunce happened.
Thus wakened I, īwis,   all wēry fordrẹmed,
And now wǫt thou my wǫ;   worde as thee līkes."

"Frēke," says the philosopher,   "thy fortūne is passed,
For thou shall find her thy fǫ;   fraist when thee līkes!
Thou art at the highest,   I hēte thee forsooth;
Challenge now when thou will,   thou chēves nǫ mǫre!
Thou has shed much blood   and shalkes destroyed,
Sakeles, in surquidrīe,   in sēre kinges landes;
3400 Shrīve thee of thy shāme   and shāpe for thīne end.
Thou has a shewing, Sir King,   tāke keep yif thee līke,
For thou shall fērsly fall   within fīve winters.
Found abbeyes in Fraunce,   the fruites are thīne ǫwen,
For Frolle and for Feraunt   and for thir fērs knightes
That thou fremedly in Fraunce   has fey belẹved.
Tāke keep yet of other kinges,   and cast in thīne herte,
That were conquerours kidd   and crowned in erthe.

"The eldest was Alexander   that all the world louted,
The tother Ector of Troy,   the chevalrous gōme;

3380 So that lady led me for the length of an hour,
with all the love and delight that a lord could desire.
But at the minute of midday her mood darkened;
she amazed me with words of malice and menace,
and when I begged for fairness her brows became enflamed.
"King, your cries are in vain, by Christ,
for all you love you shall lose, and your life as well.
You have loitered in privilege and pleasure too long."
Then she whirled the wheel about, and under it I went,
so in a moment every muscle in my body was mangled
3390 and my spine was split asunder by the seat.
Ever since this chapter I have shivered with a chill,
and awake I am wearied by the weight of the dream.
I have told of my torment, now interpret as you wish."

"Sir," said the sage, "your good fortune has ceased.
You shall find her your foe, no matter how you fight.
You sway at the summit, I swear it is so,
so challenge as you may, you will never achieve more.
You have shed much blood, butchered many beings,
killed civilians out of vanity through vast kingdoms.
3400 Now shuck off your shame and shape yourself for death.
That dream was your destiny, doubt it if you dare,
but you shall fall with great force within five winters.
Found abbeys in France—its fortunes are yours—
to Frollo and Ferrant and their fierce knights
whom you uncouthly cut down in that same country.
And heed in your heart what happened to those kings
who were called Conquerors and crowned on this earth.
The most ancient was Alexander, bowed to by all,
then Hector of Troy, that hero of high honor.

3410 The third Jūlius Cēsar, that gīaunt was holden,
In eche journee gentle, ajudged with lordes.
The fourth was Sir Jūdas, a jouster full noble,
The masterful Macabee, the mightīest of strenghes;
The fift was Josūe, that jolly man of armes,
That in Jerusalem host full much joy limped;
The sixt was David the dere, deemed with kinges
One of the doughtīest that dubbed was ever,
For hē slew with a sling by sleight of his handes
Golīas the grete gōme, grimmest in erthe;
3420 Sēnn endīted in his dayes all the dere psalmes
That in the sawter are set with selcouthe wordes.

"The tone clīmband king, I know it forsooth,
Shall Karolus bē called, the kinge son of Fraunce;
Hē shall bē crūel and keen and conquerour holden,
Cover by conquest countrees ynow;
He shall encroch the crown that Crīst bore himselven,
And that lovelich launce that lepe tō His herte
When He was crūcified on cross, and all the keen nailes
Knightly hē shall conquer tō Cristen men handes.

3430 "The tother shall bē Godfray, that God shall revenge
On the Good Frīday with galīard knightes;
Hē shall of Lorraine bē lord by leve of his fader
And sēnn in Jerūsalem much joy happen,
For hē shall cover the cross by craftes of armes
And sēnn bē crowned king with crisom annointed.
Shall no dūkes in his day such destainy happen,
Ne such mischief drīe when trewth shall bē trīed.

"For-thy Fortūne thee fetches tō fulfill the number,
Als nīnde of the noblest nāmed in erthe;
3440 This shall in romaunce bē redde with rēal knightes,

3410 The third Julius Caesar, judged a just warrior,
in battle the boldest said his brothers in arms.
The fourth was Sir Judas, a jouster and true gentleman,
and a masterful Maccabee of mighty strength.
Joshua who brought joy to Jerusalem's host
was the fifth, a fair and flawless knight.
David was the sixth, spoken of by sovereigns
as most dutiful and diligent of the knights to be dubbed,
for by skill of his hand he slew with a sling
that hulk Goliath, the most awesome on earth,
3420 then passed his days patiently composing
all the psalms in the Psalter with sacred words.
Of those two kings who clambered and climbed,
the first shall be Charlemagne, son of the French sovereign,
merciless and mighty, he shall be made a Conqueror,
capturing countless countries by combat.
He shall secure the crown worn by Christ himself,
and the lance that speared harm into our Lord's heart
while crucified on the cross; and those cruel nails
he will seek and keep safe for the sake of all Christians.
3430 The second shall be Godfrey, who in the service of God
shall bring vengeance on Good Friday with his valiant fighters.
By leave of his father he shall be lord of Lorraine,
and readily in Jerusalem joy shall be realized
for by craft of arms he will recover the cross
and be crowned the King with holy chrism.
In his day no other duke shall be dealt such destiny
nor suffer such sorrow as the story unfolds.

So fortune calls you forward to fulfil your role
and be named in the nine of the noblest on earth.
3440 Royal knights shall read this in the writings of romance:

Reckoned and rēnownd   with rīotous kinges,
And deemed on Doomesday   for deedes of armes,
For the doughtīest that ever   was dwelland in erthe;
Sǫ many clerkes and kinges   shall carp of your deedes
And keep your conquestes   in cronīcle for ever.

"But the wolves in the wood   and the wīld bęstes
Are some wicked men   that werrayes thy rewmes,
Is entered in thīne absence   tō werray thy pople,
And ālīenes and hǫstes   of uncouthe landes.
3450   Thou gettes tīdandes, I trow,   within ten dayes,
That some torfer is tidde   sēnn thou frǫ hǫme turned.
I ręde thou reckon and rehęrse   unręsonāble deedes
Ęre thee repentes full rāthe   all thy rewth workes.
Man, amend thy mood,   ęre thou mishappen,
And meekly ask mercy   for meed of thy sǫul."

Then rīses the rich king   and raght on his weedes,
A ręd acton of rǫse,   the richest of flowres,
A pesan and a paunson   and a prīs girdle;
And on hē hentes a hood   of scarlet full rich,
3460   A pavis pillion-hat   that pight was full fair
With perry of the Orīent   and precīous stǫnes;
His glōves gaylich gilt   and grāven by the hemmes
With graines of rubīes   full grācīous tō shew.
His bedē greyhound and his brand   and nǫ berne else
And bounes ǫver a brǫde męde   with brēthe at his herte.
Forth hē stalkes a sty   by tho still ēves,
Stotays at a high street,   studyand him ǫne.

At the sours of the sun   hē sees there command,
Raikand tō Rōme-ward   the rędīest wayes,
3470   A renk in a round clǫk   with right rowme clǫthes
With hat and with high shoon   hǫmely and round;

you shall be rated and reckoned by lords of rank,
and on Doomsday be worshipped for your deeds of warfare
as the worthiest warrior to dwell in the world.
So clerks and kings will declare your exploits
and in the chronicles your triumphs will be treasured for eternity.
But the wolves in the woods and the wild beasts
are the rabble of rebels who rise up in your realm,
marauding and making mayhem in your absence
with foreign hosts from far flung fields.
3450 Within ten days time you will have tidings, I tell you,
that strife has struck since you strayed from home.
I encourage you to confess all your callous crimes
or those heinous acts will return to haunt you.
Reform, before misfortune finds you, sir,
and pray you find pity for the peace of your soul."

Then the King arose and reached for his robes,
a jacket of red roses, that most royal flower,
then neck armor and body armor and a beautiful belt,
and he hauled a hood of vivid scarlet on his head
3460 and a hat from the Orient of the highest order,
studded with pearls and precious stones.
His gloves gleamed golden and the edges glinted
with grains of rubies, glorious and rare.
Then with hound and sword and no other at his side
he went fast across the fields with fury in his heart,
followed a footpath by the fringe of the forest,
then alone, by a thoroughfare, stood lost in thought.

And as the sun rose in the sky, he saw approaching,
heading toward Rome by the rapidest road,
3470 a fellow in full cloak and flowing clothes,
and a hat, and high and handsome boots.

With flat farthinges the frēke   was flourished all ọver
Many shrẹddes and shragges   at his skirtes hanges
With scrip and with sclavin   and scallopes ynow
Both pīke and palm,   als pilgrim him sholde;
The gōme graithly him grette   and bade good morwen;
The king, lọrdly himself,   of lāngāge of Rōme,
Of Latin corrumped all,   full lovely him mẹnes:
"Wheder wilnes thou, wye,   walkand thīne ọne?
3480   Whīles this world is o war,   a wāthe I it họld;
Hēre is an enmy with họst,   under yon vīnes;
And they see thee, forsooth,   sọrrow thee betīdes;
But if thou have condeth   of the king selven,
Knāves will kill thee   and keep at thou haves,
And if thou họld the high way,   they hent thee alsọ,
But if thou hāstily have help   of his hende knightes."

        Then carpes Sir Craddok   tō the king selven:
"I shall forgive him my dẹde,   sọ mē God help,
Any gōme under God   that on this ground walkes!
3490   Let the keenest come   that tō the king lọnges,
I shall encounter him as knight,   sọ Crīst have my sọul!
For thou may nọt rẹche mē   ne arrest thyselven,
Thọugh thou bē richly arrayed   in full rich weedes;
I will not wọnde for nọ war   tō wend where mē līkes
Ne for nọ wye of this world   that wrọught is on erthe!
But I will pass in pilgrimāge   this pās tō Rōme
Tō purchāse mē pardon   of the Pọpe selven,
And of the paines of Purgatory   bē plēnerly assoilled;
Then shall I seek sēkerly   my soveraign lọrd,
3500   Sir Arthur of England,   that avenaunt berne!
For hē is in this empīre,   as hathel men mē telles,
Họstayand in this Orīent   with awful knightes."

        "Frọ whethen come thou, keen man,"   quọd the king then,
"That knọwes King Arthur   and his knightes also?

Flattened farthings were affixed to him all over;
his hems were hung with tassels and trimmings,
and with his purse and skirted mantle, and scallop shells by the score,
and his staff and his palm, he appeared to be a pilgrim.
The man's greeting was a grand, "Good morning,"
and our Sovereign responded in rough Roman speech,
gave a lordly reply in the language of Latin.
"Wayfarer, why are you wandering here alone
3480 with the whole world at war? Be warned, there is danger.
An enemy army is hidden within that vineyard,
and I swear, if they spot you, sorrow will be yours.
Unless you come with safe conduct from the King himself
knaves will knife you and leave you with nothing,
and if you hold to this highway they won't hesitate to ambush you,
unless his honored knights are on hand to help."

  Then Sir Craddock spoke to the King himself:
"I shall forgive him my death, so help me God,
any warrior who walks in this world under Him.
3490 If the King's fiercest fighter should fly at me in combat
I would encounter him courteously, so Christ have my soul.
And you yourself shall not stall or stop me,
for all you are arrayed in such rich robes.
No war could deter me from wandering where I wish
and no knight either who makes his home on this earth.
So on this path I will pass on my pilgrimage to Rome
to purchase a pardon from the pope himself
and be purified to be spared the pains of purgatory.
Then I shall seek out my Sovereign lord at the soonest,
3500 Sir Arthur of England, that excellent King,
for he is actually in this empire, so I hear from true men,
at arms in the east with his eager knights."
"Where have you come from," the King questioned,
"to know of King Arthur and his noble knights?

Was thou ever in his court   whīles hē in kith lenged?
Thou carpes sǫ kindly   it comfortes mīne herte!
Well węle has thou went   and wīsely thou seekes,
For thou art Breton berne,   as by thy brǫde spēche."

"Mē ǫught tō knǫw the king;   hē is my kidd lǫrd,
3510 And I was called in his court   a knight of his chāmber;
Sir Craddok was I called   in his court rich,
Keeper of Caerlīon,   under the king selven;
Now I am chāsed out of kith,   with care at my herte,
And that castel is caught   with uncouthe lēdes."

Then the comlich king   caught him in armes,
Cast off his kettle-hat   and kissed him full soon,
Said: "Welcome, Sir Craddok,   sǫ Crīst mot mē help!
Dęre cosin of kind,   thou cǫldes mīne herte!
How fares it in Bretain   with all my bǫld bernes?
3520 Are they brittened or brint   or brǫught out of līfe?
Ken thou mē kindly   what cāse is befallen;
I keep nǫ crēdens tō crāve;   I knǫw thee for trew."

"Sir, thy wardēn is wicked   and wīld of his deedes,
For hē wandreth has wrǫught   sēnn thou away passed.
Hē has castels encrǫched   and crownd himselven,
Caught in all the rentes   of the Round Tāble;
Hē devīsed the rewm   and dęlt as him līkes;
Dubbed of the Denmarkes   dūkes and erles,
Dissevered them sonderwīse,   and citees destroyed;
3530 Of Sarazenes and Sessoines   upon sēre halves
Hē has sembled a sorte   of selcouthe bernes,
Soveraignes of Surgenale   and soudēours many
Of Peghtes and paynims   and prōved knightes
Of Ireland and Argyle,   outlawed bernes;
All thǫ laddes are knightes   that lǫng tō the mountes,

Did you call on him at court when he lodged in his country?
The way of your words brings warmth to my heart.
Your wanderings are worthwhile, and you seek wisely,
for your tongue tells me you are a true British knight."

"I should know the King, he is my noble kinsman,
3510 and I was chosen in his court as a knight of his chamber,
Sir Craddock I was called in his royal company,
his trusted captain at the castle of Caerleon.
Now I'm chased from my country with a chill in my heart,
and those battlements are seized by bandits from abroad."

Then our kind King clasped him in his arms,
cast off his kettle hat and kissed him courteously.
"Sir Craddock, by Christ you are welcome," he cried.
"But kindred cousin, you bring cold to my heart.
How goes it in Britain with my brave brothers?
3520 Are they butchered or burned, or broken from life?
Describe, in good faith, how fate unfolded.
What you tell me I shall trust, for I know you to be true."
"Sir, your warden has been wild and unwarranted in his deeds,
and has worked great wickedness since you went away.
He has captured castles and wears the crown of the King,
and the revenues of the Round Table he has raided for himself.
He has taken all the territories and partitioned them at will,
dubbing and making dukes of the dreaded Danes
who sacked and destroyed many cities as they spread.
3530 With Saracens and Saxons signed up on every side
he has assembled a great army of enemy hosts:
sovereigns of Surgenale and mercenary soldiers;
Picts, pagans, and proven knights
of Ireland and Argyll, and outlaws of the Highlands.
Every upstart from the uplands is operating as a knight

And lęding and lǫrdship has all,   als themselve līkes;
And there is Sir Childrik   a chēftain hǫlden,
That ilke chevalrous man,   hē charges thy pople;
They rob thy religīous   and ravish thy nunnes
3540 And rędy rīdes with his rout   tō raunson the poor;
Frǫ Humber tō Hawyk   hē hǫldes his ǫwen,
And all the countree of Kent   by covenant entailled,
The comlich castles   that tō the crown lǫnged,
The holtes and the hǫre wood   and the hard bankes,
All that Hengest and Hors   hent in their tīme;
At Southampton on the sę   is seven scǫre shippes,
Fraught full of fērs folk,   out of fer landes,
For tō fight with thy frap   when thou them assailes.
But yet a word, witterly,   thou wǫt nǫt the worst!
3550 He has wedded Waynor   and her his wīfe hǫldes,
And wonnes in the wīld boundes   of the west marches,
And has wrǫught her with chīld,   as witness telles!
Of all the wyes of this world,   wǫ mot him worthe,
Als wardēn unworthy   women tō yēme!
Thus has Sir Mordred   marred us all!
For-thy I merked ǫver these mountes   tō męne thee the sooth."

    Then the burlich king,   for brēthe at his herte
And for this booteless bāle   all his blee chānged;
"By the Rood," says the roy,   "I shall it revenge!
3560 Him shall repent full rāthę   all his rewth workes!"
All weepand for wǫ   hē went tō his tentes;
Unwinly this wīse king   hē wākenes his bernes,
Clēped in a clarīoun   kinges and other,
Calles them tō counsēl   and of this cāse telles:
"I am with tręsoun betrayed,   for all my trew deedes!
And all my travail is tint,   mē tides nǫ better!
Him shall torfer betīde   this tręsoun has wrǫught,
And I may traistely him tāke,   as I am trew lǫrd!

and is leader and lord to act as he likes.
And Sir Childrick is chosen as one of his chieftains,
who exploits and oppresses your people with his pack:
they rob your monks and ravage your nuns
3540 and pounce on the poor, pillaging and plundering.
From the Humber to Hawick the upper hand is his.
All the countryside of Kent is assigned to his keep—
every kingly castle which belonged to the crown,
and its copses and wild woods and the walls of its white cliffs,
all that Hengest and Horsa held in their era.
In the Solent off Southampton stand seven score ships
filled with fierce folk from foreign lands
who will attack your troops the moment you return.
But one more word, for worse news follows:
3550 he has wedded Guinevere and declares her his wife,
and his domain is the margins of the western marches,
and he has got her with child, so the gossip goes;
more than anyone on earth may woe be to him,
that regent not worthy to watch over women.
Thus Sir Mordred has marred and demeaned us all,
so I trekked across the mountains to tell you this truth."

Then the honored King, with ire in his heart
at this fall in fortune, lost all color in his face.
"By the Rood," said the royal, "I shall reap my revenge.
3560 He shall repent and pay for his faithless plotting."
And weeping with woe he went to his tents.
Then the wise Monarch woke his sleeping warriors,
roused them with a clarion, kings and every rank,
called them to council and recounted the tale:
"Despite my true deeds I am betrayed with treason,
all my actions were for nothing and my efforts led nowhere.
This treacherous villain will be trounced by trouble
once I track him to his lair, as I am a true lord.

This is Mordred, the man   that I most traisted,
3570 Has my castels encroched   and crownd himselven
With rentes and riches   of the Round Tāble;
Hē māde all his retinūes   of renayed wretches,
And devīsed my rewm   tō dīverse lordes,
Tō soudēours and Sarazenes   out of sēre landes!
Hē has wedded Waynor   and her tō wīfe holdes,
And a chīld is y-shāped,   the chaunce is no better!
They have sembled on the se   seven score shippes,
Full of ferrom folk   tō fight with mīne one!
For-thy tō Bretain the brode   buske us behooves,
3580 For tō britten the berne   that has this bāle raised.
There shall no freke men fare   but all on fresh horses
That are fraisted in fight   and flowr of my knightes.
Sir Howell and Sir Hardolf   hēre shall beleve
Tō bē lordes of the lēdes   that hēre tō mē longes;
Lookes intō Lumbardy   that there no lēde chānge,
And tenderly tō Tuskānē   tāke tent als I bid;
Receive the rentes of Rōme   when they are reckoned;
Tāke sēsin the sāme day   that last was assigned,
Or elles all the hostāge   withouten the walles
3590 Bē hanged high upon height   all holly at ones."

      Now bounes the bold king   with his best knightes,
Gars trumpe and trusse   and trīnes forth after,
Turnes through Tuskānē,   tarrīes but little,
Lights not in Lumbardy   but when the light failed;
Merkes over the mountaines   full marvēlous wayes,
Ayers through Almaine   ēven at the gainest
Ferkes ēven intō Flandresh   with his fērs knightes.
Within fifteen dayes   his fleet is assembled,
And then hē shope him tō ship   and shounes no lenger,
3600 Sheeres with a sharp wind   over the shīre waters;

And truly this is Mordred, the man I most trusted!
3570 He has captured my castles and crowned himself King,
and revels in the revenues of the Round Table.
He has formed a retinue from wretches and renegades
and divided my lands among dubious lords,
among Saracens and foreign soldiers of fortune.
And he has wedded Guinevere and boasts she is his bride,
and if he fathers a child then our fortune falls further.
On the sea are assembled seven score ships
full of foreign foe to fight with my forces.
So to Britain the Great we must go at great speed,
3580 to punish this impostor who has put us in peril.
Only fighters whose horses are fresh will follow,
and those hardened by action, my most honored men.
Sir Howell and Sir Hardolf shall remain behind
to be lords of the lands that belong to my name.
In Lombardy be alert to any change of allegiance
and in Tuscany attend to my task with attention.
Raise rent and revenue from Rome as falls due;
take possession of the city on the day that was assigned,
or those hostages we hold shall be hanged high
3590 from its outer walls, all of them at once."

Then the bold King made busy with his best knights,
and at the blaring of a bugle the party departed.
They tracked through Tuscany never tarrying on the trek,
and only lingered in Lombardy when the light was lost.
They marched over mountains, through marvelous passes,
strode through Germany, steering a straight route,
then moved forward into Flanders, that fearsome force.
Within fifteen days his fleet was fully fitted,
and soon he set sail, delaying not a second,
3600 shearing through sharp winds and shining waves.

By the roche with rǫpes   hē rīdes on anker.
There the false men flēted   and on flood lenged,
With chēf chaines of charre   chocked tōgeders,
Charged ēven chock-full   of chevalrous knightes;
Hatches with hęthen men   hęled were there-under,
And in the hinter on height,   helmes and crestes
Proudlich pourtrayed   with painted clothes,
Ęch a pēce by pēce   prikked til other,
Dubbed with dagswainnes   doubled they seem;
3610   And thus the derf Denmarkes   had dight all their shippes,
That nǫ dint of nǫ dart   dęre them sholde.

Then the roy and the renkes   of the Round Tāble
All rēaly in ręd   arrayes his shippes;
That day dūcherīes hē dęlt   and dubbed knightes,
Dresses dromoundes and dragges   and drawen up stǫnes;
The top-castels hē stuffed   with toiles, as him līked;
Bendes bǫwes of vīse   brǫthly there-after;
Toloures tently   tackle they righten,
Brāsen hędes full brǫde   busked on flǫnes,
3620   Graithes for garnisons,   gōmes arrayes,
Grim gǫdes of steel,   gīves of īron;
Stighteles steren on steren   with stiff men of armes;
Many lovelich launce   upon loft standes,
Lēdes on lēburd,   lǫrdes and other,
Pight pavis on port,   painted shēldes,
On hīnder hurdace on height   helmed knightes.
Thus they shiften for shottes   on thǫse shīre strandes,
Ilke shalk in his shroud,   full sheen were their weedes.

The bǫld king is in a barge   and about rǫwes,
3630   All bare-hęvede for besy   with bęveren lockes,
And a berne with his brand   and an helm bęten,
Menged with a mauntelet   of mailes of silver,

With ropes, by the rock face, he rode at anchor;
his fiendish foe were afloat on the flood
with ships that were shackled with chariot chains
and full to the brim with fierce fighters:
heathens hunkered under every hatch.
Riding high at the rear, crests and helmets
were proudly depicted on painted cloths,
all pinned together piece by piece
in firm fabrics so their size seemed fuller.
3610 Thus the dreaded Danes had dressed their vessels
so no darting arrow could hit or hurt them.

Then our Ruler, robed in royal red,
arrayed the Round Table's ranks in their ships.
That day he dubbed knights and dealt out dukedoms,
had his boats and barges dredge up small boulders,
stretched out many slings in the topcastle to his suiting,
and all crossbows were bent back, primed for battle.
Those attending the catapults tautened the tackle,
jagged bronze heads were joined to the projectiles,
3620 gear for the garrisons was gathered up and stockpiled—
piercing steel pikes and sturdy iron staffs.
On stern after stern stood strong men of arms
with their sleek lances lifted aloft.
Lords and other men were lined up leeward
with painted shields in place on the portside,
while high on the hind decks stood helmeted knights.
So they shifted for position on the shining sea,
and each man in his gear and his garb seemed to glow.

Our brave King was rowed back and forth in his barge,
3630 bareheaded for battle with his beaver-colored locks;
a servant bore his sword and his beaten-steel helmet
with its splendid mantle set with silver mail,

Compast with a coronal   and covered full rich;
Kaires tō ęch a cogge   tō comfort his knightes;
Tō Clēgis and Clēremond   hē crīes on loud:
"Q Gawain! Q Galyran!   Thēse good mens bodīes!"
Tō Lot and tō Līonel   full lovely hē męles,
And tō Sir Launcelot de Lāke   lǫrdlich wǫrdes:
"Let us cover the kith,   the cǫste is our ǫwn,
3640   And gar them brǫthelich blenk,   all yon blood-houndes!
Britten them within bōrde   and brin them there-after!
Hew down hertily   yon hęthen tīkes!
They are harlotes half,   I hēte you mīne hand!"

    Then hē coveres his cogge   and catches on anker,
Caught his comlich helm   with the clēre mailes;
Buskes banners on brǫde,   bęten of gules,
With crowns of clēre gold   clęnlich arrayed;
But there was chǫsen in the chēf   a chalk-whīte maiden,
And a chīld in her arm   that Chēf is of hęven;
3650   Withouten chānging in chāse   thēse were the chēf armes
Of Arthur the avenaunt,   whīles hē in erthe lenged.

    Then the mariners męles   and masters of shippes;
Merrily īch a mate   męnes til other;
Of their termes they talk,   how they were tidd,
Tǫwen trussel on trete,   trussen up sailes,
Bęte bonnetes on brǫde,   bettred hatches;
Braundisht brown steel,   brāgged in trumpes;
Standes stiff on the stamin,   steeres on after,
Streken over the stręme,   there strīving beginnes.
3660   Frǫ the wāggand wind   out of the west rīses,
Brǫthly bessomes with birr   in bernes sailes,
Węther bringes on bōrde   burlich cogges,
Whīles the biling and the bęme   bristes in sonder;
Sǫ stoutly the fore-stern   on the stam hittes

encompassed with a coronal, exquisitely crafted.
He sailed by each ship, stirring men's souls,
and to Clegis and Cleremond he cried out loudly,
"Be guided by the greatness of Gawain and Galyran!"
To Lot and Lionel and Lancelot of the Lake
he announced these noble words as he neared them:
"We shall conquer this country whose coasts are our own,
3640   and the blood of those dogs shall drain in dread;
butcher them on the boats then burn their bodies,
hew out their hearts, those heathen hounds,
they are the issue of harlots, now be led by my hand!"

     Then he boarded his own warship and weighed anchor,
donned his shining helmet with the shimmering mail,
and unrolled and raised up his royal-red banners
gloriously crafted with crisp golden crowns.
But in pride of place on his shield shone a Maiden
with an infant in Her arms, the most honored in all heaven,
3650   for through chase and challenge his faith was unchanged;
such was Arthur's honesty while he lived on this earth.
Then the mariners and the masters of the ships shouted out,
and mate called to mate with mirth in their voices,
stating how things stood and what lay in store.
They tugged on the trusses and tightened the sheets,
hoisted up bonnet sails and battened the hatches,
brandished bright swords and filled their trumpets with breath,
stood proudly at the prow and steered from the stern,
striking across waves to where the strife would start.
3660   When a wild, gusty wind rose out of the west
each blast and bluster made the sails bulge,
and the storm caused ship to slam against ship
so that bilge and beam were broken apart,
and prows and sterns were pounded and struck

That stockes of the steer-bōrde   strīkes in pēces!
By then cogge upon cogge,   crayers and other,
Castes crēpers on-cross,   als tō the craft lǫnges;
Then was hẹd-ropes hewen,   that hēld up the mastes;
There was contek full keen   and cracking of shippes!
3670 Grẹte cogges of kemp   crashes in sonder!
Many cabane clēved,   cābles destroyed,
Knightes and keen men   killed the bernes!
Kidd castels were cǫrven,   with all their keen wēpen,
Castels full comlich   that coloured were fair!
Up-tīes edgeling   they ochen there-after;
With the swing of the sword   sways the mastes,
Ǫver-falles in the first   frēkes and other;

      Many frēke in the fore-ship   fey is belẹved!
Then brǫthly they beker   with bustous tackle;
3680 Brushes bǫldly on bōrde   brenyed knightes,
Out of bǫtes on bōrde,   was busked with stǫnes,
Bẹte down of the best,   bristes the hatches;
Some gōmes through-gird   with gǫdes of īron,
Gōmes gaylich cledde   englaimes wēpenes;
Archers of England   full ẹgerly shootes,
Hittes through the hard steel   full hẹrtly dintes!
Soon ochen in hǫlly   the hẹthen knightes,
Hurt through the hard steel,   hẹle they never!
Then they fall to the fight,   foines with spẹres,
3690 All the frekkest on front   that tō the fight lǫnges,
And ilkon freshly   fraistes their strenghes,
War tō fight in the fleet   with their fell wēpenes.
Thus they dẹlt that day,   thir dubbed knightes,
Til all the Dānes were dẹde   and in the deep throwen!
Then Bretons brǫthly   with brandes they hewen;
Lẹpes in upon loft   lǫrdlich bernes;

till the planks to the starboard side were in pieces,
and cog after cog, and cutters and skiffs,
cast grapples across, as the occasion required.
Then head ropes were hewn which held up the masts,
and vessels were crippled as they crashed and cracked.
3670 Great ships of war shuddered and shattered,
many cabins were smashed and cables cleaved.

Then knights and fierce fighters killed their foe,
and topcastles were torn down with terrifying weapons,
those prominent towers which were so proudly painted.
With a sideways slash they scythed at the stays
so each swing of the sword made the mainmast sway
and the first one to topple fell on many fellows
so men at the fore went to meet their maker.
They battled bitterly with brutal weaponry;
3680 then assailing sailors swarmed onto warships
from nearby boats, and were bombarded with stones,
but beat back brave men and broke through the hatches.
Some ardent heroes, for all their fine armor
were slotted on iron spikes and made the weapons slimy.
The English archers let fly eagerly,
and their arrows struck harm through the hardest steel,
and so wholly hurt were the heathen knights,
with their armor holed, that they would never be healed.

Then our forces came forward in the fight with spears,
3690 with those famed for their fierceness surging to the front,
every man there making the most of his might
in that war on the water, with their fatal weapons.
Thus they dealt that day, those newly dubbed knights,
till all the Danes were dead and thrown in the deep.
Then the Britons broke out and went battling ahead,
swooping on noble sailors with their swords,

When lēdes of out-landes   lẹpen in waters,
All our lọrdes on loud   laughen at ọnes!

     By then spẹres were sprongen,   spalded shippes,
3700 Spanīoles speedily   sprented ọver-bōrdes;
All the keen men of kemp,   knightes and other,
Killed are cọld-dẹde   and casten ọver-bōrdes;
Their swyers swiftly   has the swẹt lẹved;
Hẹthen hẹvand on hatch   in thir hawe rīses,
Sinkand in the salt sẹ   seven hundreth at ọnes!
Then Sir Gawain the good,   hē has the gree wonnen,
And all the cogges grẹte   hē gāve tō his knightes.
Sir Garin, Sir Griswold,   and other grẹte lordes;
Gart Galuth, a good gōme,   gird off their hẹdes!
3710 Thus of the false fleet   upon the flood happened,
And thus thēse ferin folk   fey are belẹved!

     Yet is the traitour on land   with trīed knightes,
And all trumped they trip   on trapped steedes
Shews them under shēld   on the shīre bankes;
Hē ne shuntes for nọ shāme   but shewes full high!
Sir Arthur and Gawain   avyed them bọthen
Tō sixty thousand of men   that in their sight hōved.
By this the folk was felled,   then was the flood passed;
Then was it silke a slowde   in slackes full huge
3720 That let the king for tō land   in the lọw water.
For-thy hē lenged on laye   for lēsing of horses,
Tō look of his lēge-men   and of his lēle knightes,
Yif any were lāmed or lost,   live yif they sholde.

     Then Sir Gawain the good   a galley hē tākes
And glīdes up at a gole   with good men of armes;
When hē grounded, for grēf   hē girdes in the water
That tō the girdle hē gọes   in all his gilt weedes,

and when those warriors from other lands leapt to the water
all our lords began laughing out loud at once.

By now spears were splintered and ships were shattered;
3700 Spaniards had sprung smartly over the side;
many keen and courageous knights and their comrades
were killed cold dead and cast into the deep,
squires lay squashed, their lifeblood squandered,
heathens jumped in horror as the ocean heaved
and sank in the salt sea, seven hundred at a stroke.
So good Sir Gawain had grabbed the prize,
and all those grand galleys he granted to his generals—
Sir Garyn, Sir Griswold and other great lords.
With honorable Galuth he beheaded his enemies.
3710 So the foe's fleet floundered on the floodtide,
and all those false foreigners were flung to their fate.

Yet the traitor was on land, with tried and trusted knights,
trotting about in their trimmings to the blowing of trumpets,
on the shimmering shore with their shining shields,
and Mordred did not shrink but showed himself without shame.
Then King Arthur and Gawain looked onward together
and saw sixty thousand soldiers marching into sight.
Many fellows had been felled and the floodtide had ebbed,
and now the channels were so silted and swampy with sludge
3720 that in such low-lying water the King was loathe to land,
so stayed at sea to save his steeds from the quicksand,
and look after his liegemen and loyal knights
so the lives of the lamed might be saved and not lost.

Then good Sir Gawain took charge of a galley
and glided up a gulley with a group of armed men;
where he went aground he waded through the water,
walked girdle deep in his gleaming gold garb,

Shootes up upon the sand   in sight of the lordes,
Singly with his soppe,   my sorrow is the more!
3730 With banners of his badges,   best of his armes,
Hē braides up on the bank   in his bright weedes;
Hē biddes his bannēour: "Busk thou belīve
Tō yon brode batail   that on yon bank hōves,
And I ensūre you soothe   I shall you sew after;
Look yē blenk for no brand   ne for no bright wēpen,
But beres down of the best   and bring them o-dawe!
Bēs not abaist of their boste,   abīde on the erthe;
Yē have my banneres borne   in batailes full hūge;
Wē shall fell yon false,   the fēnd have their soules!
3740 Fightes fast with the frap,   the fēld shall bē oures!
May I that traitour over-tāke,   torfer him tīdes
That this tresoun has timbered   tō my trew lord!
Of such a engendūre   full little joy happens,
And that shall in this journee   bē judged full ēven!"

        Now they seek over the sand,   this soppe at the gainest,
Sembles on the soudēours   and settes their dintes;
Through the shēldes so sheen   shalkes they touch
With shaftes shivered short   of those sheen launces;
Derf dintes they delt   with dāggand speres;
3750 On the dank of the dew   many dede ligges,
Dūkes and douspeeres   and dubbed knightes;
The doughtīest of Danemark   undōne are forever!
Thus those renkes in rewth   rittes their brenyes
And reches of the richest   unrecken dintes,
There they throng in the thick   and thrustes tō the erthe
Of the throest men   three hundreth at ones!
But Sir Gawain for grēf   might not again-stand,
Umbegrippes a spere   and tō a gōme runnes,
That bore of gules full gay   with goutes of silver;
3760 Hē girdes him in at the gorge   with his grim launce

and strode onto the sand in sight of those lords,
just himself and his entourage, though it hurts me to say so.
3730　With his bold heraldic banners and his best arms
he bounded up the banking in his bright colors,
and to his banner bearer he said, "Go briskly
at that broad battalion massed on the embankment,
and by my faith I shall follow at your feet;
see you swoon from no sword nor shrink from any weapon,
but drag down the doughtiest and deliver them from daylight.
Don't be intimidated by their taunts but stand tall.
You have borne my banners in many a great battle,
we shall fell those false men, and let the Fiend have their souls.
3740　Fight fiercely with this foe and the field shall be ours.
Should I overturn him, woe betide the traitor
who contrived a treason against my true lord.
Out of such circumstances any joy will be scant
as the fight to follow will confirm without doubt."

　　Then that band of stalwarts streamed across the strand,
tearing at those troops and attacking with intent,
piercing men's skin through their shining shields
and splintering lances with spikes and spears.
Fatal wounds they fetched with their fearful weapons,
3750　till many lay dead in the damp of the dew:
dukes and nobles and newly dubbed knights,
Denmark's most daunting, were forever undone.
In rage, our ranks went on ripping and riving,
slashing at the strongest with unstoppable strokes
and thrusting to the earth in the thick of the throng
the most thorough warriors, three hundred at a throw!
And Gawain, in his ire, could not harness his anger,
but swiped up a spear and went speeding at a soldier
bearing splendid scarlet spotted with silver;
3760　with his lance he thrust right through him at the throat,

That the grounden glaive   graithes in sonder;
With that bustous blāde   hē bounes him tō dīe!
The King of Gotheland it was,   a good man of armes.
Their avauntward then all   voides there-after,
Als vanquist verrayly   with valīant bernes;
Meetes with middle-ward   that Mordred lędes;
Our men merkes them tō,   as them mishappened,
For had Sir Gawain the grāce   tō hǫld the green hill,
Hē had worship, īwis,   wonnen forever!

3770   But then Sir Gawain, īwis,   hē waites him well
Tō wręke on this warlaw   that this war mōved,
And merkes tō Sir Mordred   amǫng all his bernes,
With the Montagūes   and other gręte lǫrdes.
Then Sir Gawain was grēved   and with a gręte will
Fewters a fair spęre   and freshly ascrīes:
"False fostered fōde,   the fēnd have thy bǫnes!
Fy on thee, felon,   and thy false workes!
Thou shall bē dęde and undōne   for thy derf deedes,
Or I shall dīe this day,   if destainy worthe!"

3780   Then his enmy with hǫst   of outlawed bernes
All enangles about   our excellent knightes
That the traitour by tręsoun   had trīed himselven;
Dūkes of Danemark   hē dightes full soon,
And lęders of Lettow   with lēgīons ynow,
Umbelapped our men   with launces full keen,
Soudēours and Sarazenes   out of sēre landes,
Sixty thousand men,   seemlyly arrayed,
Sēkerly assembles there   on seven score knightes,
Sodēnly in dischaite   by thǫ salt strandes.
3790   Then Sir Gawain grette   with his grey eyen
For grēf of his good men   that hē guīde sholde.
Hē wiste that they wounded were   and wēry for-fǫughten,

so the honed spear point splintered on impact
and from that lusty blow the man lost his life.
It was the King of Gotland, a great man of combat.
The remaining foe seemed to flee from the field,
vanquished by the verve of valiant knights,
who moved now on the middle ranks commanded by Mordred,
our men marching to meet them, and more was the pity,
for had Gawain made ground and gained the green hill
his success had been certain and assured forever.

3770   But Gawain in his wisdom watched and waited
to root out the wrongdoer whose unruliness led to war,
and through the mass of his men he made for Sir Mordred,
with the Montagues at his side and other mighty soldiers.
Sir Gawain was furious, and by the force of his will
he leveled a long lance and bellowed loudly:
"False bastard beast, let the Fiend have your bones.
Foulness upon you, felon, and your fake ways.
For your undignified deeds you shall drop to your death,
or I shall die this day, if my destiny is to do so."

3780   Then his enemy and his host, that hired army,
ensnared our excellent knights in a circle,
who were tricked and trapped by that treacherous traitor.
Dukes of Denmark were quick to do their duty,
and leaders from Lithuania with their many legions,
surrounding our soldiers with their spears at the ready;
outlaws and Saracens from over the ocean,
sixty thousand warmongers lying in wait,
came swooping swiftly on our seven score knights
in sudden deceit by the salt-laden sea.
3790   Then Gawain's gray eyes were wet with weeping
out of grief for the good men he had guided thus far,
for he saw they were wounded and wearied by war,